Research/Practice 02

Research/Practice 02

Heba Y. Amin

The General's Stork

Edited by
Anthony Downey

Sternberg Press

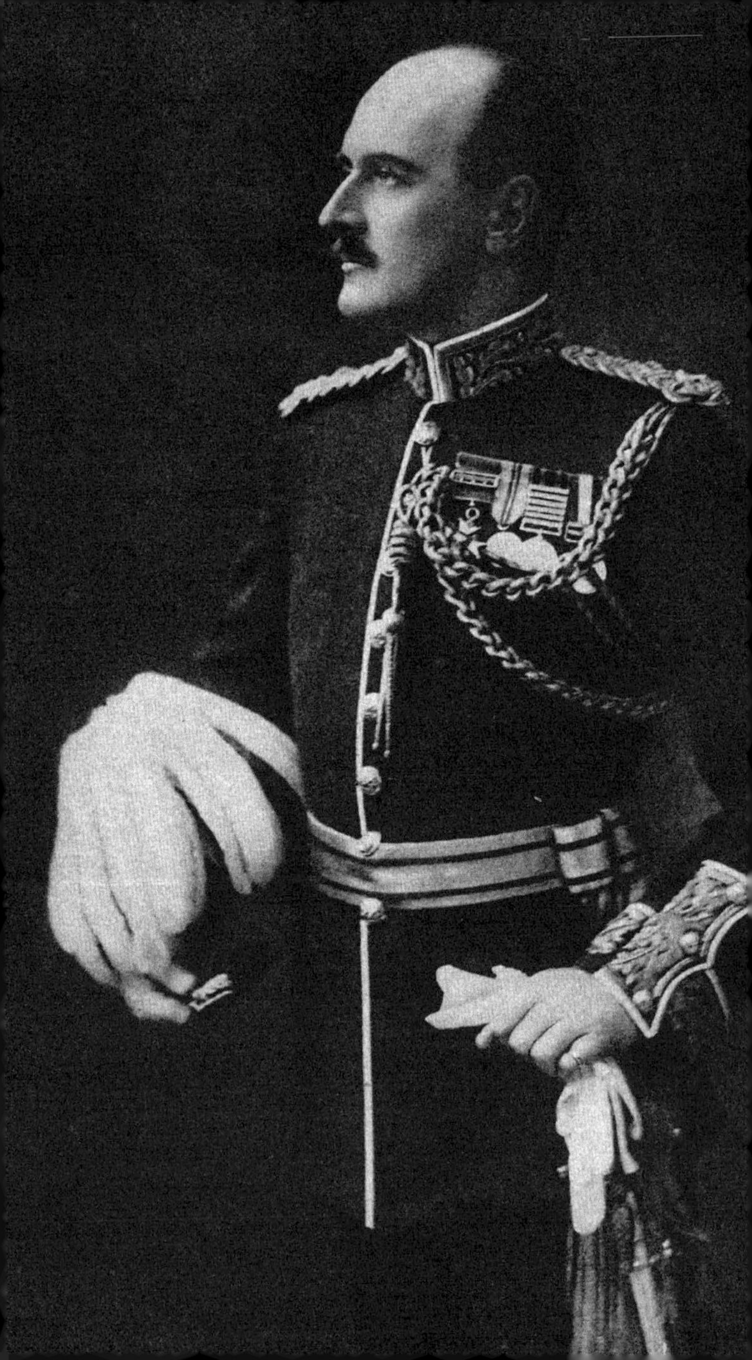

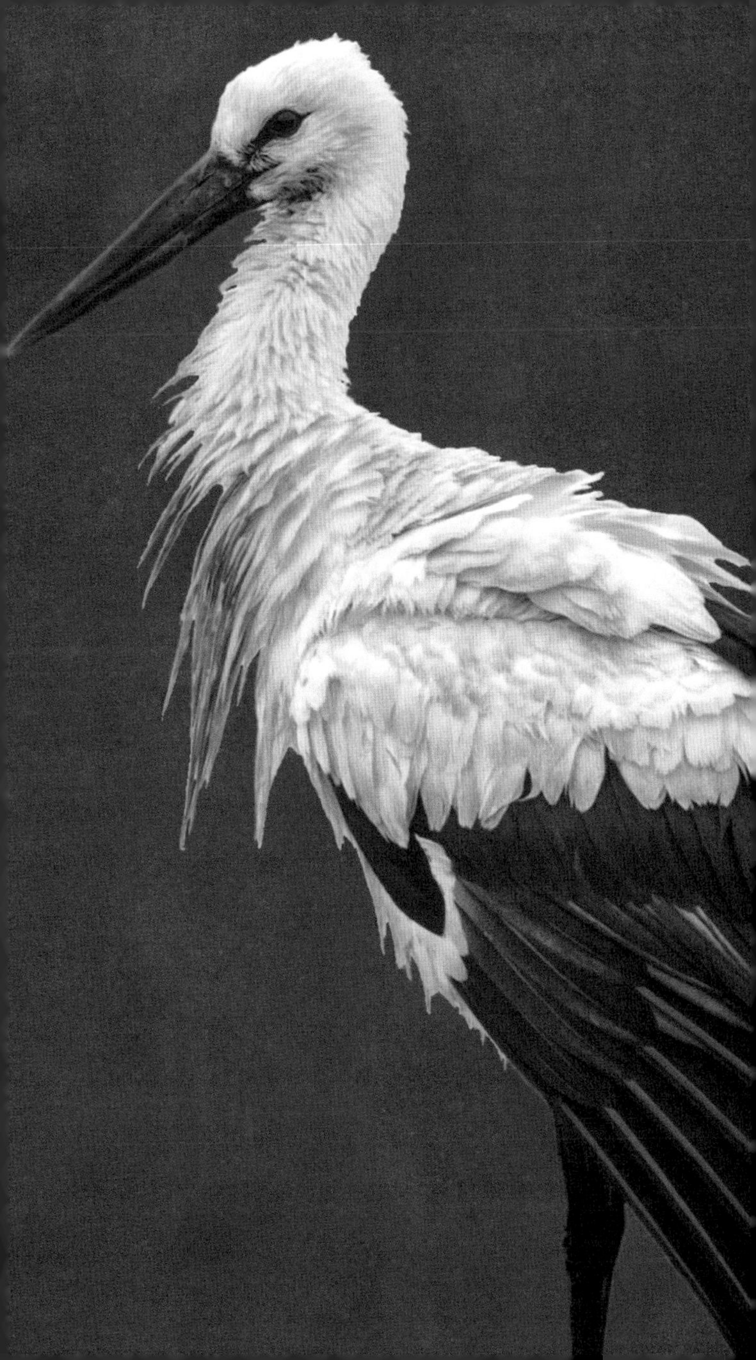

Contents

There's Always Someone Looking at You

Performative Research and the Techno-Aesthetics of Drone Surveillance[1]

Anthony Downey

"What are those?" asked the camera operator.
"Women and children," the Predator's mission intelligence coordinator answered.
"That lady is carrying a kid, huh? Maybe," the pilot said.
"The baby, I think, on the right. Yeah," the intelligence coordinator said.
—Transcript of a Predator drone strike in Uruzgan Province, Afghanistan, February 21, 2010

Technology is far ahead of humanity and ethics.
—Jonas Mekas

In September 2013, Egyptian authorities detained a migratory stork that had arrived in Egypt after traveling from Hungary via, among other countries, Israel. Reportedly captured by a fisherman who viewed the bird with suspicion after noticing an electronic device attached to it, the unfortunate stork was handed over to the local police station in Qena (a city situated on the east bank of the Nile in Upper Egypt). A police report was filed, and the bird was interned. Upon further investigation, it transpired that the "camera device" was, in fact, a functioning tracking instrument attached by Hungarian scientists who were researching avian migratory habits. Through an intercession by Nature Conservation Egypt (NCE), the stork, called Menes, was released into a nature reserve. According to Haitham Mossad, an ornithologist and member of NCE, Menes flew to an island on the Nile where he was reportedly caught and eaten. NCE subsequently released a statement lamenting the bird's demise: "We truly are saddened by the tragic end to Menes' journey, but once again, we would like to thank the park rangers of Aswan for their excellent initial efforts to get Menes the White Stork released safely into a protected area."[2]

This was not the first time an animal had been suspected of espionage, nor was it the only instance. The list is long and includes: fourteen squirrels captured in Iran in 2007 while apparently attempting to infiltrate the country with "spy gear"; two pigeons, supposedly loitering with intent around a uranium enrichment plant, again in Iran, in 2008; an errant vulture detained in 2011 by Saudi authorities on suspicion that it was flying missions for Israel; a bird captured in Sudan in 2012, also accused of spying for Israel; and a vulture tagged for tracking by Tel Aviv University and detained in 2016 in Lebanon when its GPS transmitter raised concerns that it was an agent for Mossad, the Israeli national intelligence agency.

Given that post-2011 Egypt was in the grip of momentous change in terms of its social, economic, cultural, and political circumstances, the story of Menes could be perhaps best understood as an all too acute reminder of the psychological condition of a nation, if not region, that perpetually exists in a heightened state of suspicion when it comes to external forces and, indeed, internal machinations.[3] This event might be therefore peremptorily dismissed as an example of rampant paranoia, overzealousness, and xenophobia. However, as Heba Y. Amin's project *The General's Stork* (2013–ongoing) amply reveals, this apparently bizarre tale reveals something far more profound, not least the ubiquitous shadow of surveillance that prevails over the Middle East in respect of the latent and yet all too real threat of death and injury hailing from the skies above.

The apparent incongruity of indicting or holding a stork responsible for the crime of espionage, as Amin's research astutely uncovers, initially became an expedient way for Western media outlets—which have long had an antagonistic relationship with the region—to highlight what they considered to be both the ridiculousness of the situation and the gullibility of those involved. A spying stork, as Adel Iskandar observes in this volume, "perpetuates the existing narrativization of absurdity around Egypt," and confirms for some the tendency to "see Egypt as a place where strange, mystical things happen and people behave in illogical ways." In an age of social-media communication and targeted disinformation, where a Twitter spiel can go viral regardless of its veracity, the yarn of the luckless stork was simply too good to turn down. *The General's Stork* offers a more nuanced interpretation of those events that avoids reducing the headline-grabbing tale of Menes's demise to a simple fable of xenophobia (or, indeed, ornithophobia or zoophobia). Amin proposes that what happened in this supposedly ludicrous moment readily exposes and lays bare the far from amusing geopolitics of the region—in both its antagonisms and affiliations—and the historical ascendancy of drone surveillance in automated warfare.[4] Her project also addresses one of the key concerns surrounding the legacy of Orientalism and how digital technologies have further secured and recalibrated the West's "imaginative command," to use Edward Said's perspicacious phrase, while, in turn, producing an image regime that renders the entire region—from Pakistan to Libya and beyond—in terms of atavistic threat and belligerent insurgency.[5]

Scopic Regimes and Digital Warfare

In 1917, the British High Commissioner of Egypt, Lord Edmund Allenby (1861–1936), purportedly instigated his own attempt to fulfill a biblical prophecy. The prophecy to which Allenby, a devout Christian, was apparently responding to is found in Isaiah 31:5: "As birds flying, so will the Lord of hosts defend Jerusalem; defending also he will deliver it; and passing over he will preserve it." Interpreting this as a somewhat anachronistic reference to airplanes, Allenby subsequently ordered a number of low-level flights over Jerusalem to drop leaflets urging its residents to surrender and avoid loss of life.[6] Allenby, as we learn in *The General's Stork*, signed these with his name in Arabic: النبي or *al naby*, which translates as the "prophet" or "son of god." The Ottoman Turks, who had ruled Jerusalem since 1517, were aware of another prophecy that proclaimed that the city would never be taken until a "man of Allah came to deliver it." As a result of this, Allenby was deemed to be precisely such a figure, so much so that the demoralized Turks surrendered the city to a Christian ruler for the first time in four centuries.

In the years leading up to Allenby's arrival in Jerusalem, other aerial-bound devices were being invented, including a form of "pigeon photography" pioneered in 1907 by Julius Gustav Neubronner (1852–1932), a German apothecary, inventor, amateur photographer, and filmmaker. As Amin recounts in *The General's Stork*, Neubronner attached a lightweight camera to a homing pigeon in the hopes that it would take photographs as it flew above cities.[7] The results were impressive and Neubronner's techniques were later employed by the Swiss clockmaker Christian Adrian Michel (1912–1980), who adapted the German's panoramic camera to 16 mm film and enhanced it with a clockwork delay mechanism to control the timing of exposures.[8] Successive advances in aviation technology and photography, which caught the attention of the German army in the 1930s, led to substantial developments in imaging and reconnaissance during the Second World War, where aerial photographs were used to determine troop movements and to plan military attacks.[9] The concepts behind Neubronner's ideas, by way of Michel and others, are today considered forerunners of mechanized drones or unmanned aerial vehicles (UAVs) and the armed reconnaissance drones that emerged in the 1980s.[10]

A line can be drawn here from Neubronner's pigeons to Michel's clockwork inventions and the ascendancy of automated drones. In the context of Menes's story and the then fractious political climate in Egypt in 2013, it becomes evident that fear of aerial surveillance has become an integral part of the pathology of airspace as it is experienced across vast areas of the Middle East. The sky has become a place from which subjects—often viewed as objects—are scrutinized, categorized, and in some cases targeted (and potentially eliminated) as so-called enemy combatants. In the ostensible absurdity of a bird being arrested, we glimpse the impending menace of the drone. This scenario is made all the more believable by the fact that drone design, as Amin observes, has recently resorted to the science of ethology—the study of animal behavior, specifically the aerodynamics of flight—to perfect UAVs that resemble birds. Allenby's protective birds, the biblical augury of both refuge and threat, metamorphize here into the spectre of approaching death-by-drone.

It is difficult to determine the exact numbers of those killed in the Middle East by drone strikes, due to the secrecy and sensitivities surrounding their use; however, it is known that such strikes increased tenfold under the presidency of Barack Obama. Resulting in somewhere between an estimated 384 and 807 civilian deaths, across Pakistan, Somalia, and Yemen in particular, it has been reported that during Obama's two terms as president—January 20, 2009, to January 20, 2017—there were 563 drone strikes in comparison to the 57 strikes ordered under George W. Bush's tenure.[11] To effect such loss of life does not necessarily involve someone on the ground who is in possession of firsthand knowledge of the terrain or full demographics of the region; rather, death is delivered remotely, from afar, and from the safety of one of the US Air Force bases that discretely dot the hinterlands of New Mexico, Texas, Florida, California, Nevada, and other highly classified sites.[12] Information from drones deployed across the Middle East, Afghanistan, and Pakistan is typically relayed via satellites to these air-force bases where drone operators make decisions—such as whether to fire a Hellfire II anti-armor missile from a Predator drone—based on the theoretical and qualitative (as opposed to definitive and quantitative) information that is received.[13] And this is where the problems begin: theory, based on technologies that visually enhance the terrain below, is an a priori way of deducing reality from hypotheticals; or, more simply put, the drone operator is not experiencing a firsthand reality but making a decision based on statistical probability and risk assessment (not to mention their conjectural backfilling of what they can and cannot see), which can in turn determine the difference between life and death.[14]

The vectors of engagement here—ranging from partial information sourced on the ground, digitized data from drones, satellite imaging from airspace, and human input from an army base located in the United States—are supposed to seamlessly connect within a system that can deduce reality and thereafter eliminate "combatants" and other threats, while also ensuring no resulting danger to either the drone operator or, supposedly, anyone deemed a "noncombatant." The reality is often not only far from this neatly plotted arc of military-command structures, but is also sometimes in direct, inevitably injurious if not fatal, contradistinction to it.[15] Being seen, whether you are a combatant or a noncombatant, is equivalent to courting death—and the central element here involves the technological manifestation, or operation, of a digital image that gives both form and appearance to a subject (target). This is the domain of techno-aesthetics, where the correlation between utility—or, to use Harun Farocki's phrase, "operational images"—and reality (appearance) becomes potentially lethal.[16] In this scopic, invariably inequitable, regime of observation and transmission, the techno-aesthetics of drone surveillance, despite the obvious epistemic dilemmas—*how do we know what we know and by what means do we know it*—that attend the technology involved, fatally dovetails with the necropolitical and terminal logic of digital warfare.[17] Or, as Martin C. Libicki succinctly puts it, in this ascendant paradigm of perceptibility and exposure "visibility equals death."[18]

The surveying, mapping, and bombing processes involved in drone warfare are approximate—virtual and abstract in aesthetic and actual terms—and yet have real-life, often calamitous, repercussions. We need to ask, therefore, what exactly constitutes the substantive nature of the images being produced and who decides on their veracity, not least when their apparent "truth" can predicate death? In some instances, drone operators, carried away with the "unreality" of it all and likening their activities to gaming, imagine (through digital imaging) nefarious activities where they do not exist. An overactive imagination, despite training, can yield death. Disregarding the potential impact of a missile on actual people (as opposed to digitized abstractions), drone operators often go ahead and give orders that result in mutilation, disfigurement, and multiple civilian casualties.[19] This has produced, over time, a collective mistrust of what might come from the skies and what could potentially happen to those who dwell beneath its firmament.

If we consider the documentation for *The General's Stork* alongside the performative presentation of

Amin's findings, then it is notable that the research methodologies employed owe, in part at least, something to investigative journalism.[20] Given the subject matter in hand, this is no doubt appropriate: we are, after all, considering matters of life and death. To this end, there is also a circumstantial evidentiary context being developed throughout this research, whereby a case of sorts is being made and a method of investigative analysis is being promoted. This point is expanded upon in the conversation in this volume between Amin and the filmmaker Laura Poitras, where the latter notes how often the material she uncovers becomes "newsworthy" and subsequently referenced by legislative and political agents: "I've been interested in that as a methodology and partly as a strategy, because institutions don't always feel comfortable talking about classified information. In other words, we can launch something in the news at the same time as we put it in the museum." In this context, Amin's project tends to methodically engage with historical material—be it allegorical, apocryphal, evidentiary, virtual, or otherwise—and subject it to a speculative model of inquiry *within* the cultural context of a museum or gallery. Bearing this in mind, Amin's investigative, speculative research *is* her artistic practice. Revealing as it does the symptoms of widespread paranoia (not least a bird accused of spying), *The General's Stork* draws on multidisciplinary fields of inquiry—including digital optics, the technology of warfare, colonial and neocolonial history, the contemporary politics of warfare, techno-aesthetics, data analytics, ordinance mapping, and, of course, ethology and ornithology—to effect an exploratory cultural treatise on the historical prevalence of surveillance technology and the techno-aesthetic regime that has been brought to bear on how the Middle East is visualized. Thereafter, such material can indeed become newsworthy in its own right, inasmuch as it relates to the realities of drone-ordained life and death in the Middle East.[21]

The globalized presence of the digitized gaze, defined by the ubiquity of the drone and made manifest in the techno-aesthetics of the images produced as a result of its operations, is not only a deterrent (being watched promotes normative behavioral patterns, however surreptitious they might turn out to be), it is also a means to subjugate and define subjects in prohibitive, proscribed terms. Drone surveillance has ushered in its own techno-aesthetic realm for producing the realities of the Middle East—in both subjective and objective terms—based on rampant suspicion and intrinsic fear, not to mention the premonition of retaliation.[22] This logic is, of course, historically embedded in a martial framework, whereby the ambition to disambiguate the distinction between combatant and noncombatant is linked to improved processes of killing.[23] To see is to capture and to be rendered visible is to be bound to death.

In this sense, the allegorical and metaphorical meaning of the term "scoping," a word that has a number of interlinked meanings that range from active looking (or reconnaissance) to how we might, through strategic farsightedness, better identify and eradicate an enemy, becomes more obvious. A scope is a material entity that can represent, in its suffix form (-scope), both an instrument utilized for looking and the act of looking at, if not capturing, the object of the gaze.[24] In referring to that which is aimed at or desired, or the objective that one wishes to effect or attain, this calculated elision between the actual instrument and the object under observation enables an event of seeing that encompasses a transitive action, insofar as it is an act that is carried over from the object (scope) to the subject (that which is scoped).[25] It is an act of looking that demands an object to complete its function and ambition. This judicious conjunction between viewer, object, and the attainment of a subject through active realization—the desire to see being a desire to not only behold but hold—is a readily applicable means to understand the apparatus of surveillance and how drone technology effects a fluid movement between the viewer (in this case the gaze of the machine and, by extension, the drone operator), the object (the subject of surveillance), and the execution of a desired outcome that is often quantifiable in terms of annihilation.

The degree to which the surveillance technologies associated with satellites and drones continue to be developed, by the United States in particular, and with the Middle East in mind, discloses yet another element in the otherwise poignant tale of Menes: the region known to us as the "Middle East" is not only a readily discernible historical construct, but it has been largely created to conform to the unyielding and obsessive gaze of Western-centric imaging systems and the distrustful imaginations of neo-imperial ideologues. The means by which this gaze produces the Middle East as a site of repressed desire, recurrent threat, and imminent terror have shifted in time from the relatively analogue processes behind photographic and filmic representation to the digitized technologies of drone surveillance. The imaging and imagining of the region have also evolved in both intent and outcome. Whereas, in its historical and ideologically driven intent, the embodied gaze of the camera-eye produced an image intended for the human eye to view, those forms of corporeally invested observation have been augmented since by a closed, autonomous method of scrutiny, whereby machines generate images that are only ever viewed by other machines. This is, in sum, the epoch of the machine-eye or, recalling Farocki's terminology, it is the dominion of "operational images," wherein which the Middle East is produced as both a present-day and future reality. The techno-aesthetic image, based on the utilization of operational images, not only gives form (appearance) to the Middle East but also adumbrates—presents it in outline *and* simultaneously foreshadows it—the future substance and materiality of the region's contested topographies.[26] This ultimately involves, to revisit and revise my earlier point, an automated act of looking that not only demands an object to complete its functional surveillance, but a long-term, future-oriented objective within which to fully realize its imperial ambitions.

Images made by machines for machines are not being generated to represent subjects or objects; rather, they are part of an operational, insular context that has become self-referential and self-serving. They are autonomous systems of interpretation and empirical deduction that further reveal (and enable) the collusive and corrosive representational strategies deployed by both Orientalism and, seamlessly, Neo-Orientalism. While simultaneously centralizing mechanized models of image production within the realm of unaccountable state actors, military-industrial technologies, and sovereign forms of power, these systems of image-making have given rise to an image complex that has spawned a techno-aesthetics of digital surveillance that further maintains the hegemonic ascendancy of the unseeing machine eye. And it is with this in mind that we can more fully understand the implications behind a seemingly absurd story of an unfortunate bird and his untimely demise: we no longer need to see images of the Middle East, but, if the scopic regime associated with Orientalism is to maintain its ostensibly interminable power to determine the realities of the region as a whole, we do need machines to see them.

Algorithmic Anxieties and the Future of Death

In the context of the techno-aesthetics produced by UAVs, drone warfare not only generates a psychopathological relationship to airspace based on anxiety, fear, and trepidation, but also consigns and delivers the Middle East to new forms of visibility and visualization to combat such fears. Conflict, in this reciprocal logic, is viewed as a region-wide phenomenon capable of emerging from anywhere and everywhere at once, while territorial control is contingent on the technological means of visualization, rather than occupation. The apparent ubiquity of hostility was a mainstay of colonial discourse, but its technological manifestation through the means of a digital eye exposes a set of circumstances whereby the techno-aesthetics of visualization—the (operational) means of envisioning and the synchronized manifestation (appearance) of the image as a targeted object—is irredeemably imbricated within a seemingly reciprocal and yet unending replay of future conflict and threat.[27]

Considering the spectacle of the first Gulf War in 1991 (as it was presented through videos of "smart bombs" seeking their targets), the more recent 2003 bombings of Iraq, the use of drones during the Libyan civil war, and the intervention of drones in Syria in 2014, it is easy to see how the Middle East has become a testing ground for such image-making systems. While there are numerous points of evolution between the corporeal and the digital, future-oriented gaze of drone surveillance (between, that is, Orientalist aesthetics and the techno-aesthetics of drone surveillance), we nevertheless need to pose a crucial question: What if the techno-aesthetics produced by the machine gaze gives rise to an image of the region that—through "operational images"—is not only unhinged from the frames of reference associated with the Western image regime that underwrote colonial fantasies, but from all previously understood regimes of viewing and conceptual understanding?

In an age of networked systems of digital communication and advances in imaging techniques, drone warfare is driven by and defined through artificial intelligence (AI), augmented reality, and opaque algorithms. These technologies are increasingly produced in the realm of private companies that are vying for government-sponsored military contracts—a matter of concern that needs further attention.[28] In a military chain of command that enables fatal mistakes to enter into the process, however, faults are often attributed to "human error." Unmanned drones, already implicated in bypassing human operators, could be vastly improved by algorithmic means—or so we are told—so that human error would be eradicated. In this scenario, algorithms increasingly control death delivering missiles and consequently repudiate any moral obligation for the act of killing.[29] If we can automate the procedures involved in the empirical deduction of reality and thus, through algorithmic modification, denude the entire process of the subjective view of a human, then we not only enter the realm of "operational images," we also cross the threshold of moral and ethical culpability. If drones are producing images for other drones and machines to understand the difference between combatant and noncombatant, then the very process of imaging is self-referentially looped in a holding pattern that can endlessly replay a version of the region for the sole purposes of mass surveillance and the administration of death with impunity.

The affiliation between AI, algorithms, and drones being forged in the military-industrial and private sectors continues to give cause for concern, inasmuch as these systems enable UAVs to learn and to "think" for themselves. Powered by such technologies and relying on in-built algorithmic forms of machine-learning to function, drones can self-referentially make decisions on whether to bomb or not. Questions of advanced probability coalesce here with a risk-free, unprincipled approach to killing. Add to this the advances made in augmented reality, the blending of physical and digital environments, and we can see how a military-industrial complex can produce the very reality of a territory—through technological and ideological means—that further warrants the long-term invasion and subjugation of an entire region.[30] Algorithms, often mistakenly seen as abstract, dispassionate, and detached entities, are the product of data sets—images used to train machine-learning methods and improve algorithmic performance levels—and come complete with their own embedded biases.[31] The ensuing techno-aesthetics of digital surveillance has given rise to an ascendant topographical contouring of the Middle East—a quartering of time and space—based upon biased forms of risk assessment that can only ever reproduce nascent forms of inauspicious subjects from within the logic of an apparently unending war on terror.

Drone technology, determined by the ominous rationalizations of algorithmic bias, will not only target individuals deemed as a threat in the present, but will predefine what constitutes that threat in the future. This is the underlying principle of the techno-aesthetic command associated with the necropolitics of drone vision: it is no longer implicated in dispatching death in real time, but also in the process of preemptively marking the targets of drone-decreed death for future elimination. For Achille Mbembe, whose work on corporeality and the rationalizing logic of the necropolitical realm was alluded to earlier, necropolitics defines the right to *subject* others to death, rather than just the right to kill. This, often extrajudicial, sentence of impending if not looming death also, momentously, defines who will live. This is an important distinction as it summons up an image of the walking dead rather than the dead—a vision of a life lived in limbo awaiting preordained death that has no limits or time frame of completion other than the algorithmically impenetrable, and yet politically rationalized, demand that it be neutralized and destroyed. Political exigencies, driven by technological advances in surveillance, traduce and yet continue to determine the ethics and efficacy of death-by-drone. Mbembe writes: "In our contemporary world, weapons are deployed in the interest of maximum destruction of persons and the creation of death-worlds, new and unique forms of social existence in which vast populations are subjected to conditions of life conferring upon them the status of living dead."[32] The calibrated desire to kill, supported by algorithms and drone technologies, is implicated here in an anachronistic temporality whereby someone or something is posited as existing in a future historical order—an order of approaching death. The impulse to kill is therefore proleptic: it collapses chronology and potentially defines the future—in which death will be administered from the sky above—as having already happened. This is perhaps the fateful (fatal) logic of "operational images" and the techno-aesthetic visual complex that they give rise to: in a worst-case scenario, we will not need to see images of the Middle East, machines will do that for us, but we will also not need to contemplate images of death as they will be always forthcoming and just about to happen, somewhere out of sight but not, needless to say, out of range.

In her project, Amin repeatedly poses the following question: What is at stake in the moment of covertly and digitally representing a region that is in itself already a symptom—or mediated manifestation—of a systemic representational logic that has existed within colonial discourse since at least the eighteen century? This is not only about the future of surveillance but the future imaging of the Middle East through a system that, given its neural networks, advanced technologies, seemingly endless resources, the support of private interests (such as Microsoft, Amazon, and Google), big data, and the acceleration of AI technology, will effectively produce the image regime that will define the realities of the Middle East for generations to come. Throughout *The General's Stork* and the research that underwrites its findings, suspicions about a "spying" stork, regardless of how bizarre they may at first appear, are intimately associated with this global interlocking of surveillance technologies, territorial plotting, imperialist expansionism, and drone warfare—and these concerns, far from being regional, are at the forefront of global debates about the future of life and death in our anxious age of algorithmic reasoning.

1 This title is a reworking of The Boomtown Rats' single "Someone's Looking at You," the third and final release from their 1979 album *The Fine Art of Surfacing*. The song contains the lines: "There's a spy in the sky / There's a noise on the wire / There's a tap on the line / And for every paranoid's desire ... / There's always someone looking at you."

2 Quoted in Conal Urquhart, "Arrested 'Spy' Stork Killed and Eaten after Release in Egypt," *Guardian*, September 7, 2013, https://www.theguardian.com/world/2013/sep/07/arrested-spy-stork-killed-eaten-egypt.

3 In Egypt, such sentiments were advocated by its former president Hosni Mubarak, and later perpetuated by his replacement Mohamed Morsi, the latter being the short-lived fifth president of Egypt from June 2012 to July 2013. Since his election to the presidency in June 2014, a similar degree of guardedness and suspicion continues to be propagated by Abdel Fattah el-Sisi and the security apparatus of the Egyptian state. Morsi, who was replaced by Sisi on July 3, 2013, was jailed pending trial and later collapsed during a court hearing and died of a heart attack. He was, perhaps uncoincidentally, being held on charges of espionage.

4 This point is further reinforced when we learn, through Amin's copious research, that there is also a military site based in Qena, where we first came across Menes, that goes under the deceptively inoffensive name of Site Alpha. This was one of the military bases involved in the ill-fated attempt to free the fifty-two American diplomats and citizens who were held hostage—from November 4, 1979, to January 20, 1981—during the Iran hostage crisis. Site Alpha, Amin's research further divulges, was a former Soviet air base, a leftover from the days when the Russians and Egyptians were in a Cold War alliance of convenience based on a shared distrust of the "West" and its military ambitions in the region.

5 The colonial infiltration of the self-proclaimed "West" into the Near East and other territories, Edward W. Said argued throughout *Orientalism*, went hand in hand with the production of systems of knowledge that secured, tentatively and yet persistently, the colonizer's "imaginative command" over the colonized. This command, for Said, was systematic and irrefutably implicated European culture—during the post-Enlightenment period and thereafter—in producing, rather than reflecting on, the "reality" of the so-called Orient through political, social, militaristic, ideological, and scientific discourses. For Said, the power of this command reveals the sinuous collusion of colonial knowledge with power and, in turn, the extent to which the "authority of academics, institutions, and governments can accrue to it, surrounding it [knowledge] with still greater prestige than its practical success warrants. Most important, such texts can create not only knowledge but the very reality they appear to describe." See Edward W. Said, *Orientalism* (1978; repr. London: Routledge and Kegan Paul, 1980), 94.

6 The subject of leaflet dropping, in relation to the Middle East and beyond, is likewise the subject of Rabih Mroué's nonacademic lecture-performance *The Crocodile Who Ate the Sun* (1982/2015), in which he refers to the dropping of leaflets in Beirut in 1982 and compares it to similar instances in Japan during the Second World War and, later, in Palestine.

7 This was not the first time that airborne technology was used to photograph land and townscapes. Gaspar Felix Tournachon, commonly known as Nadar, is widely acknowledged to have taken the first successful aerial

photograph in 1858. This was done from a hot-air balloon tethered 262 feet over Petit Bicêtre, a small town outside of Paris. Later, in 1860, James Wallace Black positioned a hot-air balloon, the so-called Queen of the Air, two thousand feet above Boston. Nadar's images were lost, so Black's view of Boston is considered to be the oldest surviving aerial photograph. For a fuller account of aerial photography and its effects on how we view the world, see Paula Amad, "From God's-Eye to Camera-Eye: Aerial Photography's Post-humanist and Neo-humanist Visions of the World," *History of Photography* 36, no. 1 (2012): 66–86.

8 Michel's original plan to sell his camera to the Swiss Army was unsuccessful; nevertheless, following the outbreak of the Second World War, he went on to patent a shell and harness for the transport of items, such as film rolls, by carrier pigeon. For an overview of the variable exposure timer, in particular, its patent and design, see https://www.christies.com/LotFinder/lot_details.aspx?from=searchresults&intObjectID=4001985.

9 A more contemporary version of such practices involves the use of "intelligent drones," or, less succinctly, the deployment of albatrosses fitted with lightweight radar detection devices used to identify illegal fishing ships in remote locations. See Eleanor Ainge Roy, "'Intelligent Drones': Albatross Fitted with Radar Detectors to Spot Illegal Fishing," *Guardian*, January 31, 2020, https://www.theguardian.com/world/2020/jan/31/intelligent-drones-albatross-fitted-with-radar-detectors-to-spot-illegal-fishing.

10 These include the Predator and Reaper drones. Armed with two Hellfire air-to-surface missiles (ASM), the Predator drone has both reconnaissance and offensive capabilities. Initially developed by Abraham Karem, the former chief designer for the Israeli Air Force, the original technology for the Predator was encased in the so-called Amber drone. Karem is considered to be the founding father of UAV (drone) technology, having built his first one for the Israeli Air Force during the 1973 Arab–Israeli War. The Predator entered service in 1995 and has since been deployed in Afghanistan, Pakistan, Iraq, Yemen, Libya, Syria, and elsewhere.

11 For fuller details, see Jessica Purkiss and Jack Serle, "Obama's Covert Drone War in Numbers: Ten Times More Strikes than Bush," *Bureau of Investigative Journalism*, January 17, 2017, https://www.thebureauinvestigates.com/stories/2017-01-17/obamas-covert-drone-war-in-numbers-ten-times-more-strikes-than-bush.

12 In 2012, it was estimated that there were sixty-four drone bases in the US. See Lorenzo Franceschi-Bicchierai, "Revealed: 64 Drone Bases on American Soil," *Wired*, June 13, 2012, https://www.wired.com/2012/06/64-drone-bases-on-us-soil/.

13 Interestingly, given the allusions to aviation, Lord George Curzon, the Secretary of State for Foreign and Commonwealth Affairs of the United Kingdom (1919–24), called Afghanistan "the cockpit of Asia." See Ahmed Rashid, *Taliban* (London: Yale University Press, 2001), 7.

14 Throughout *Drone Theory*, Grégoire Chamayou notes how the supposed psychopathological effects of drone warfare—the mechanics of killing from afar—on operators located in the US, for example, has led to a process whereby the latter are supposed to suffer post-traumatic stress disorder (PTSD); however, as Chamayou further observes, such forms of psychopathologicization—

the suggestion that operators suffer, experience stress, over-empathize, and endure emotional exhaustion, fatigue, and burnout—can serve to humanize the life-or-death decisions that these operators make remotely, and thus return debates to the question of morality and suffering, albeit in respect of the drone operators rather than their targets. This sleight of hand, so to speak, can, in turn, publicly rehabilitate the ideal of homicide by drone, and further quash moral and ethical debates about the automization of death. See Grégoire Chamayou, *Drone Theory* (London: Penguin Random House, 2015), 106–13. Another recent work that examines the psychopathology of drone warfare is Omer Fast's *5,000 Feet Is the Best*, produced in 2011. For an analysis of this film in terms of labor and the bureaucratization of killing, see Peter M. Asaro, "The Labor of Surveillance and Bureaucratized Killing: New Subjectivities of Military Drone Operators," *Social Semiotics* 23, no. 2 (2013): 196–224. In what follows, I am more concerned, however, with the pathological effects of drones on those who are subject to their surveillance and threats of death.

15 The epigraph to this essay, for example, is taken from a transcript that was originally quoted in an article by David S. Cloud where he described an attack on three vehicles in the Uruzgan province of Afghanistan and the ensuing deaths of twenty-three civilians on the morning of February 21, 2010. See David S. Cloud, "Anatomy of an Afghan War Tragedy," *Los Angeles Times*, March 14, 2014, https://www.latimes.com/archives/la-xpm-2011-apr-10-la-fg-afghanistan-drone-20110410-story.html. The same events are cited at the outset of Chamayou's *Drone Theory* and, in a different context, in Lauren Wilcox's "Embodying Algorithmic War: Gender, Race, and the Posthuman in Drone Warfare," *Security Dialogue* 48, no. 1 (2016): 11–28.

16 Farocki used the phrase "operational images" to describe images made by machines for machines, the full implications of which he explored throughout his three-part film *Eye/Machine I, II, III* (2000–3). These machine-oriented images are not produced in relation to representing either subjects or objects; rather, they are part of an operation. For Trevor Paglen, writing of this phenomenon, Farocki "was one of the first to notice that image-making machines and algorithms were poised to inaugurate a new visual regime. Instead of simply representing things in the world, the machines and their images were starting to 'do' things in the world. In fields from marketing to warfare, human eyes were becoming anachronistic." See Trevor Paglen, "Operational Images," *e-flux journal*, no. 59 (November 2014), http://worker01.e-flux.com/pdf/article_8990555.pdf.

17 I draw on the phrase "necropolitics" from Achille Mbembe's eponymous essay in which he details the links that have "emerged between war making, war machines, and resource extraction." The phrase is often discussed in relation both to and in distinction from Foucault's notion of biopolitics. See Achille Mbembe, "Necropolitics," *Public Culture* 15, no. 1 (Winter 2003): 33.

18 See Martin C. Libicki, quoted in Antoine Bousquet, *The Eye of War: Military Perception from the Telescope to the Drone* (Minneapolis: University of Minnesota Press, 2018), 3.

19 There are numerous instances of civilian death by drone. Observing the deployment of drone warfare in Yemen, the US office of the Sana'a Center for Strategic Studies (SCSS) in New York has noted that "in the 15 years in which the US has deployed military drones in Yemen, there have been hundreds of civilian deaths, untold suffering endured by the injured and loved ones of the victims. This has

deeply marred the image of the United States in the eyes of Yemenis and enables recruitment for AQAP [Al Qaeda in the Arabian Peninsula]." Citing the Columbia Law School Human Rights Clinic and SCSS findings, the author of this damning report goes on to note that "the US government's figures and estimates are significantly lower [...] than those gathered by independent organizations, including those that use on-the-ground, fact-finding missions to calculate casualty figures." See Waleed Alhariri, "Country Case Study: Yemen," in *The Humanitarian Impact of Drones*, ed. Ray Acheson et al. (New York: Women's International League for Peace and Freedom, 2017).

20 I should observe here that Amin has developed a separate, more allegorical project, under the title of *As Birds Flying* (2016). This short film responds to similar issues through the use of found drone footage (including aerial views of savannas and wetlands, and settlements in Galilea), and alludes to both political corruption and religious radicalism through the use of audio sequences from Adel Emam's 1995 film *Birds of Darkness*. The militaristic connotations, against this backdrop, is further imbued in the nouns used to describe a flock—a muster of storks or a phalanx of storks—of storks and how both terms relate to a gathering of troops.

21 This was certainly the case with an earlier intervention by Amin, when she took the opportunity to subvert the graffiti used in an episode of the American spy-thriller television series, *Homeland*. See Dan Bilefsky and Mona Boshnaq, "Street Artists Infiltrate 'Homeland' with Subversive Graffiti," *New York Times*, October 15, 2015, https://www.nytimes.com/2015/10/16/world/europe/homeland-arabic-graffiti.html.

22 The missile that killed Major General Qasem Soleimani of the Iranian Islamic Revolutionary Guard Corps and commander of the Quds Force, alongside the Iraqi politician and military commander Abu Mahdi al-Muhandis and seven others, at Baghdad International Airport on January 3, 2020, was reportedly launched from an MQ-9 Reaper drone. The MQ-9, also known as Predator B, is referred to by the US Air Force as a remotely piloted vehicle/aircraft. The operation to assassinate Soleimani is believed to have been directed by the CIA from Creech Air Force Base in Nevada. See Russ Read, "World's Most Feared Drone: CIA's MQ-9 Reaper Killed Soleimani," *Washington Examiner*, January 3, 2020, https://www.washingtonexaminer.com/policy/defense-national-security/worlds-most-feared-drone-cias-mq-9-reaper-killed-soleimani.

23 The technologies being developed in relation to non-Western regions and contexts are often also being "tested" for more homegrown use. Peter Thiel, a venture capitalist and Facebook board member, founded Palantir in 2004 and developed its profile working for the Pentagon and the CIA in Afghanistan and Iraq. It has been reported that Palantir has been employing data-mining tools used in the so-called War on Terror to track American citizens. See Peter Waldman, Lizette Chapman, and Jordan Robertson, "Palantir Knows Everything about You," *Bloomberg Businessweek*, April 19, 2018, https://www.bloomberg.com/features/2018-palantir-peter-thiel/. See also Shosana Zuboff, *The Age of Surveillance Capitalism: The Fight for a Human Future at the New Frontier of Power* (London: Profile Books, 2019); and Jocelyn Wills, *Tug of War: Surveillance Capitalism, Military Contracting, and the Rise of the Security State* (Montreal: McGill–Queen's University Press, 2017).

24 The Greek term *skopos*, one of the roots of "scopic," similarly alludes to both someone watching and a target. The term and its meaning are central to Lacanian models of the subject- and object-based "scopic field." For Antoine Bousquet, writing in *The Eye of War: Military Perception from the Telescope to the Drone*, the term "scopic regime" has Cartesian roots in its "reduction of perceptual space to mathematical and homogeneous space" that gives rise—post-Renaissance and within the context of a scientific world-view of the early modern period—to a "rationalized articulation of vision and space." See Bousquet, *Eye of War*, 10.

25 In grammatical terms, a transitive verb describes an action carried from the subject to the object, but it also needs a directly defined object through which to complete its full meaning.

26 I am drawing here on the Latin root of the term "adumbrate"—namely, *umbra* or shadow—and the way in which it describes a series of activities that include giving an outline or form to an object through foreshadowing or casting a shadow upon it.

27 The relationship between drone technologies, gaming, and entertainment, noted earlier in connection to the augmented realities that power the gaming industry and the way in which Hollywood normalizes the wish list of the US military-industrial complex, can be further progressed here if we consider that so-called "instant replay" was introduced in 1963 during an American college football game. Invented by Tony Verna, the first instant replay showed a touchdown, from a different camera angle, moments after it had been broadcast live. The subsequent use of the technology involved gave rise to replays in slow motion from multiple camera angles, freeze-frame shots, frame-by-frame review, variable speed replay, overlaying of graphics, and instant analysis tools. In 2008, it was reported that the US military uses the same video technology the National Football League uses for instant replay to analyze video from drones. See Michael Grotticelli, "Military Uses Instant Replay Technology in Afghanistan," *TV Technology*, July 9, 2010, https://www.tvtechnology.com/miscellaneous/military-uses-instant-replay-technology-in-afghanistan.

28 There are multiple connections to be had between social-media companies such as Google, Facebook, Microsoft, and others, and the US military-industrial complex, none of which should come as a surprise given that the precursor to the internet was Arpanet, a communication system developed in the US in the 1960s as an early warning system for the nuclear age. For a review of Google's involvement in drone technology, see Lee Fang, "Google Hired Gig Economy Workers to Improve Artificial Intelligence in Controversial Drone-Targeting Project," *Intercept*, February 4, 2019, https://theintercept.com/2019/02/04/google-ai-project-maven-figure-eight/. For details of the US government's Project Maven and Google's role in its development, see Lee Fang, "Google Is Quietly Providing AI Technology for Drone Strike Targeting Project," *Intercept*, March 6, 2018, https://theintercept.com/2018/03/06/google-is-quietly-providing-ai-technology-for-drone-strike-targeting-project/. For an overview of Amazon's concerted efforts to enter into the national security market contracts of the United States, see Sharon Weinberger, "The Everything War," *MIT Technology Review* 122, no. 6 (November/December 2019): 26–29. Amazon's cloud-based software program Rekognition is also used for the purpose of facial recognition by a number of US government agencies including the US Immigration and Enforcement agency. More recently, it was announced that Peter Thiel, mentioned above in relation to Palantir, was one of the financial backers of

Clearview AI, a privately owned facial-recognition app that has been deployed, without any public scrutiny as to potential misuse and its future weaponization by authoritarian governments, by over six hundred law enforcement agencies across the US. See Kashmir Hill, "The Secretive Company That Might End Privacy as We Know It," *New York Times*, January 18, 2020, https://www.nytimes.com/2020/01/18/technology/clearview-privacy-facial-recognition.html.

29 Debates about whether drone-based targeted killing programs are indicative of an incipient moral indifference to death, caused by armed conflict in particular, are widespread within military, ethical, and legal fields. See Michael J. Boyle, "The Legal and Ethical Implications of Drone Warfare," *International Journal of Human Rights* 19, no. 2 (2015): 105–26; Anders Henriksen and Jens Ringsmose, "Drone Warfare and Morality in Riskless War," *Global Affairs* 1, no. 3 (2015): 285–91; and Bradley Jay Strawser, "Moral Predators: The Duty to Employ Uninhabited Aerial Vehicles," *Journal of Military Ethics* 9, no. 4 (2010): 342–68.

30 It was recently reported that the US Army is developing a program called the Integrated Visual Augmentation System, which adapts a version of Microsoft's augmented-reality headset—the latter being a self-contained holographic computer—to provide more effective modes of night vision, thermal sensing, and monitoring of vital signs. See Julia Carrie Wong, "'We Won't Be War Profiteers': Microsoft Workers Protest $480m Army Contract," *Guardian*, February 22, 2019, https://www.theguardian.com/technology/2019/feb/22/microsoft-protest-us-army-augmented-reality-headsets.

31 The issues of algorithmic bias in racial profiling and the politics of inequality have been explored in, respectively, Safiya Umoja Noble, *Algorithms of Oppression: How Search Engines Reinforce Racism* (New York: New York University Press, 2018); and Virginia Eubanks, *Automating Inequality: How High-Tech Tools Profile, Police, and Punish the Poor* (London: St. Martin's Press, 2018).

32 See Mbembe, "Necropolitics," 40.

Pages 32–39: First aerial photographs of Palestine, ca. 1900–20: (in order) Olivet Range from 4,500 meters, Jericho Road from 3,000 meters, Bethlehem from 3,000 meters, and Nazareth and environs from 2,500 meters.

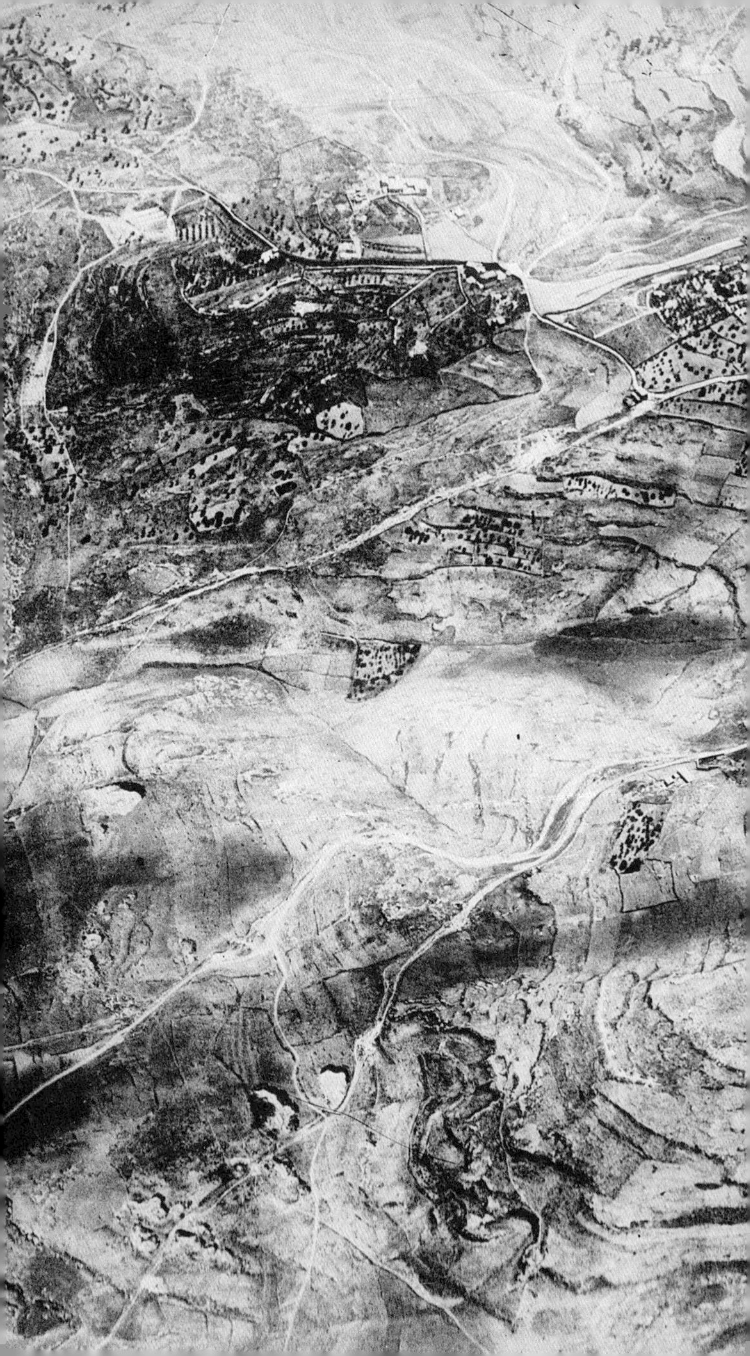

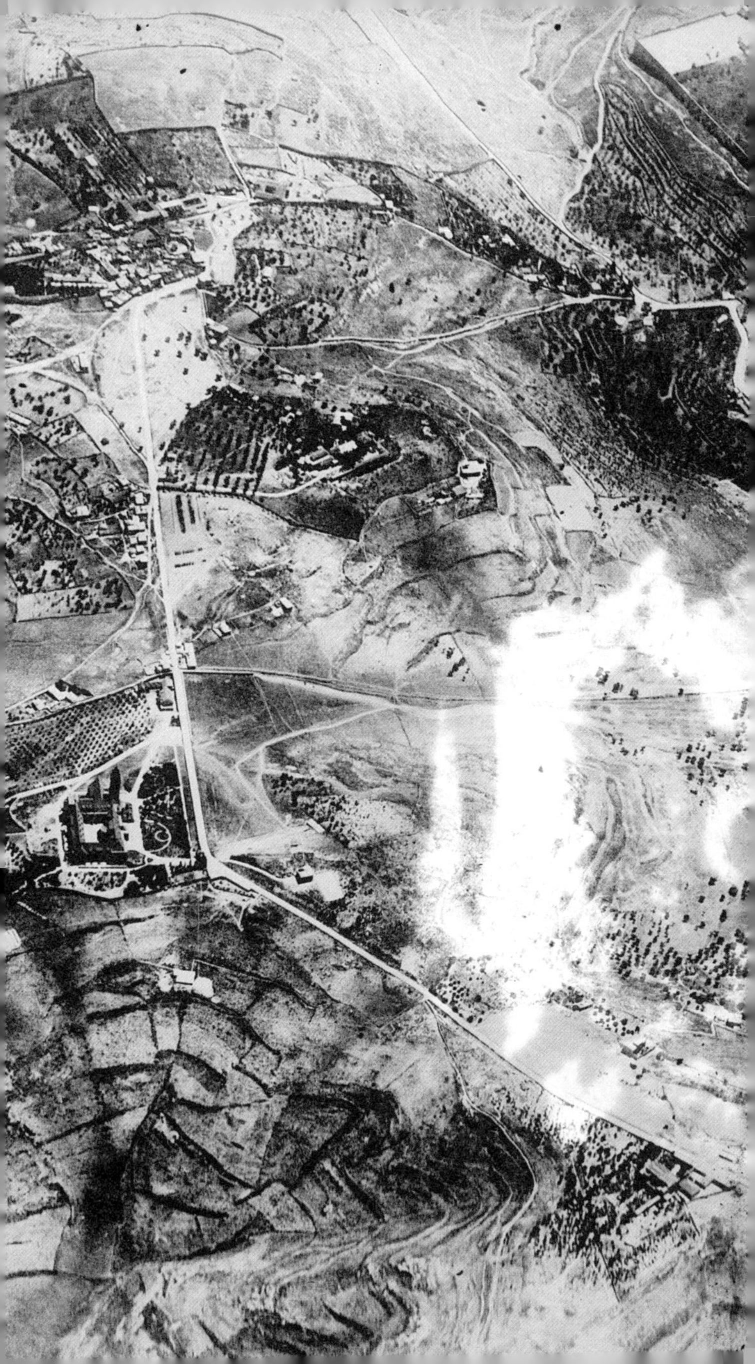

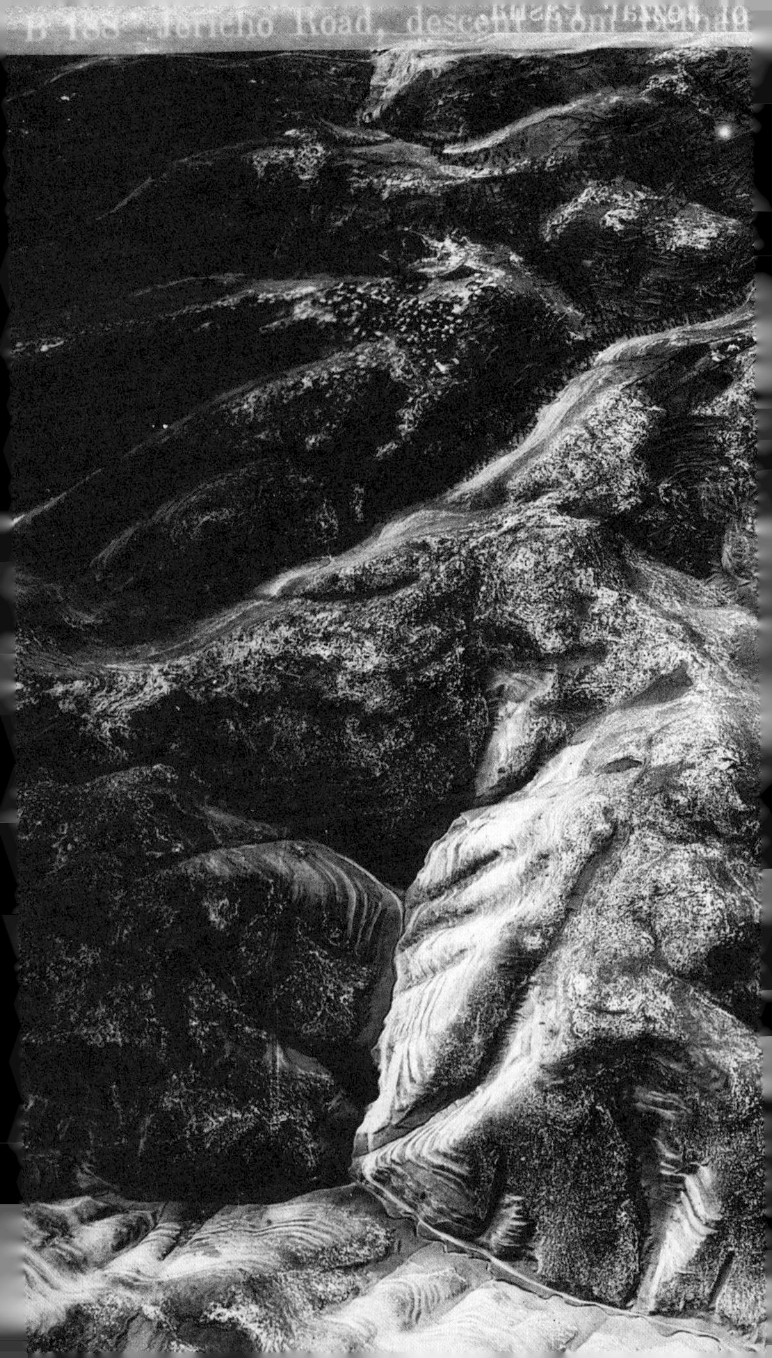
B 188 Jericho Road, descent from Bethany

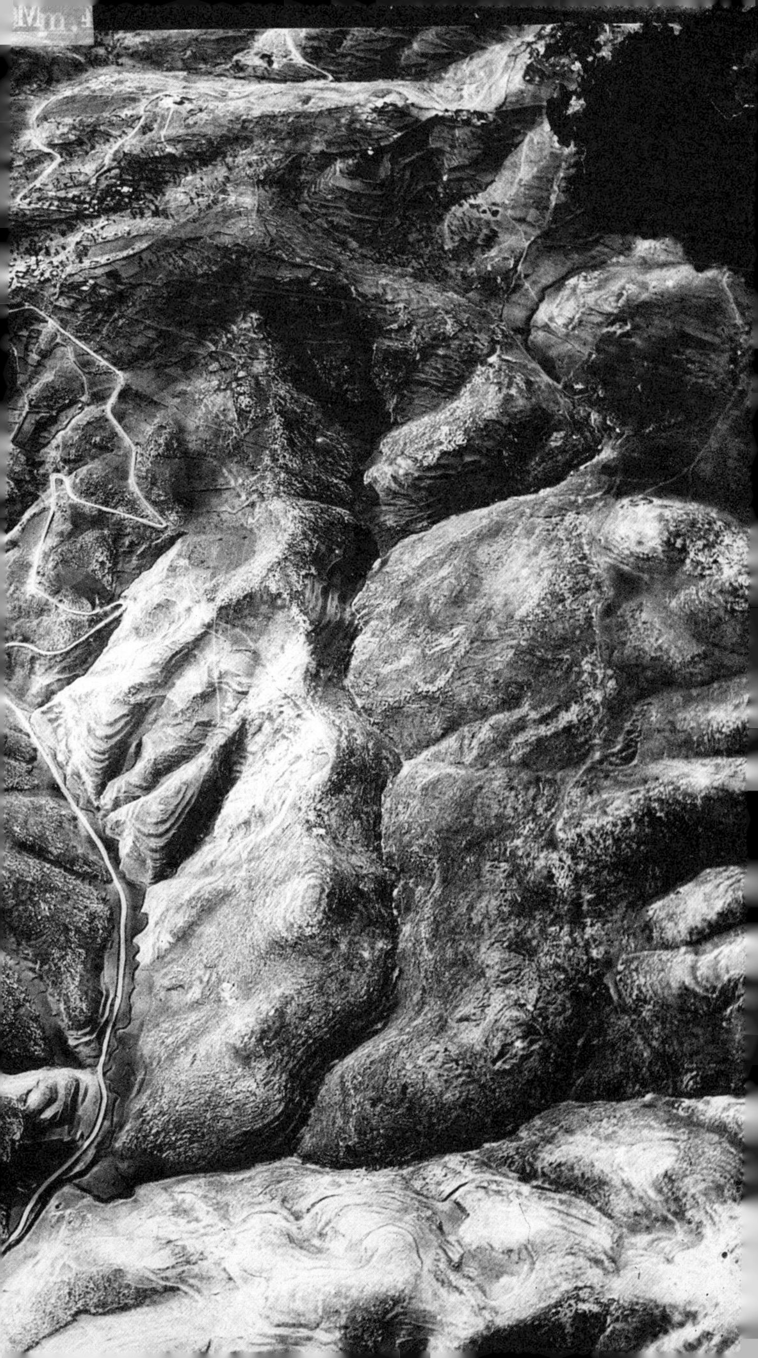

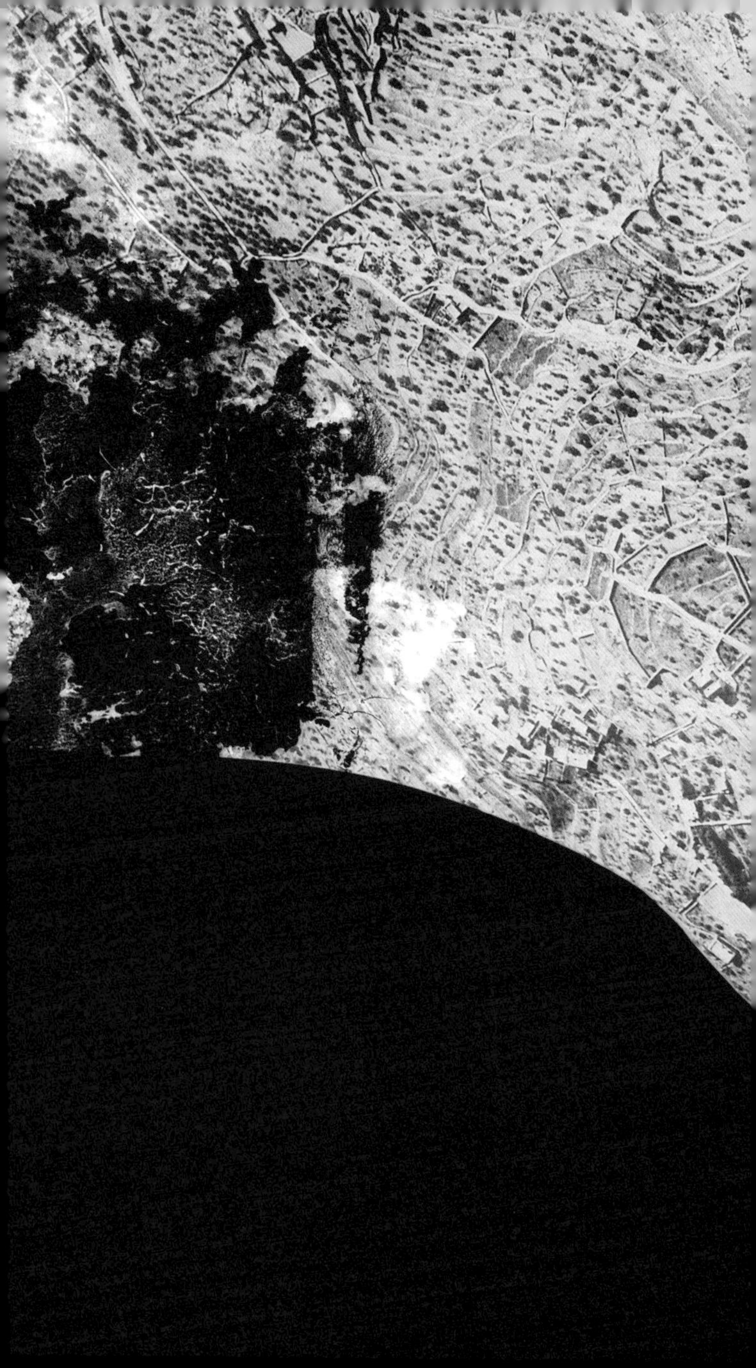

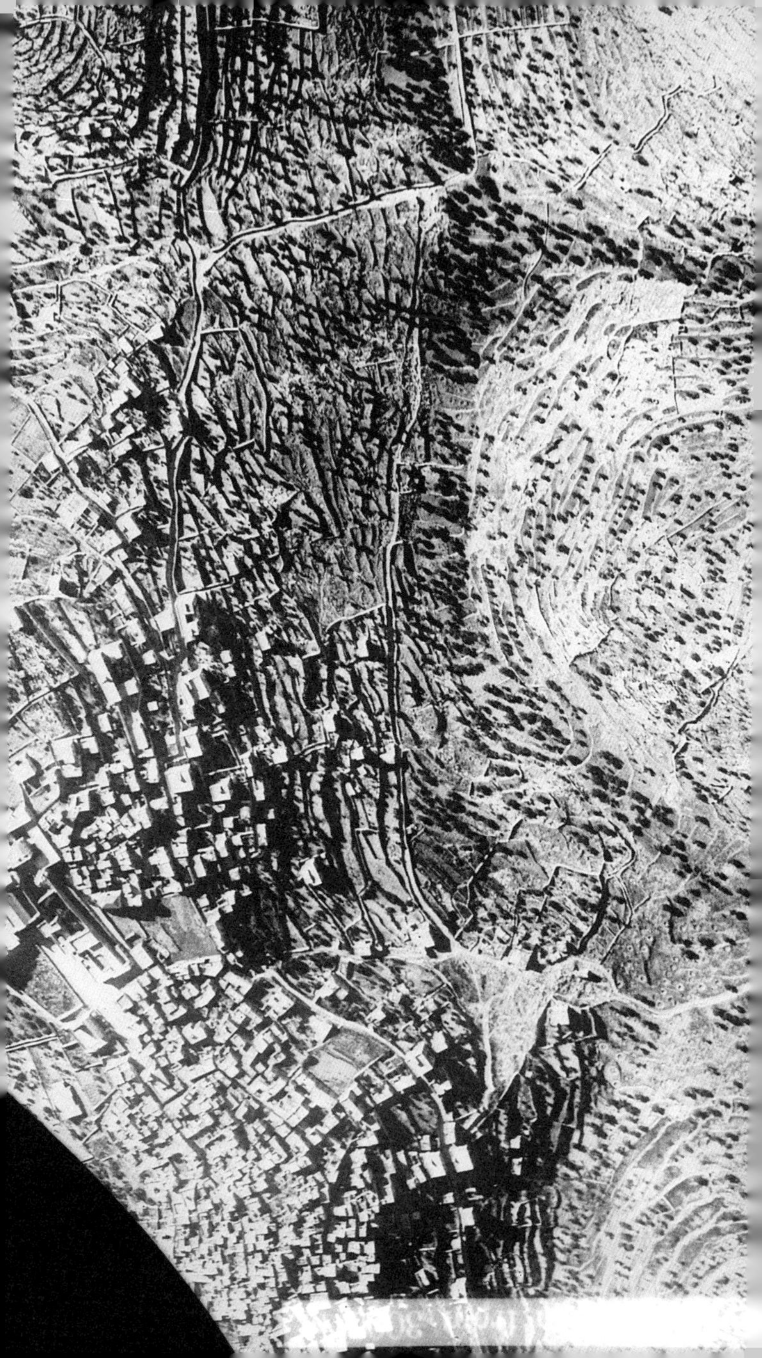

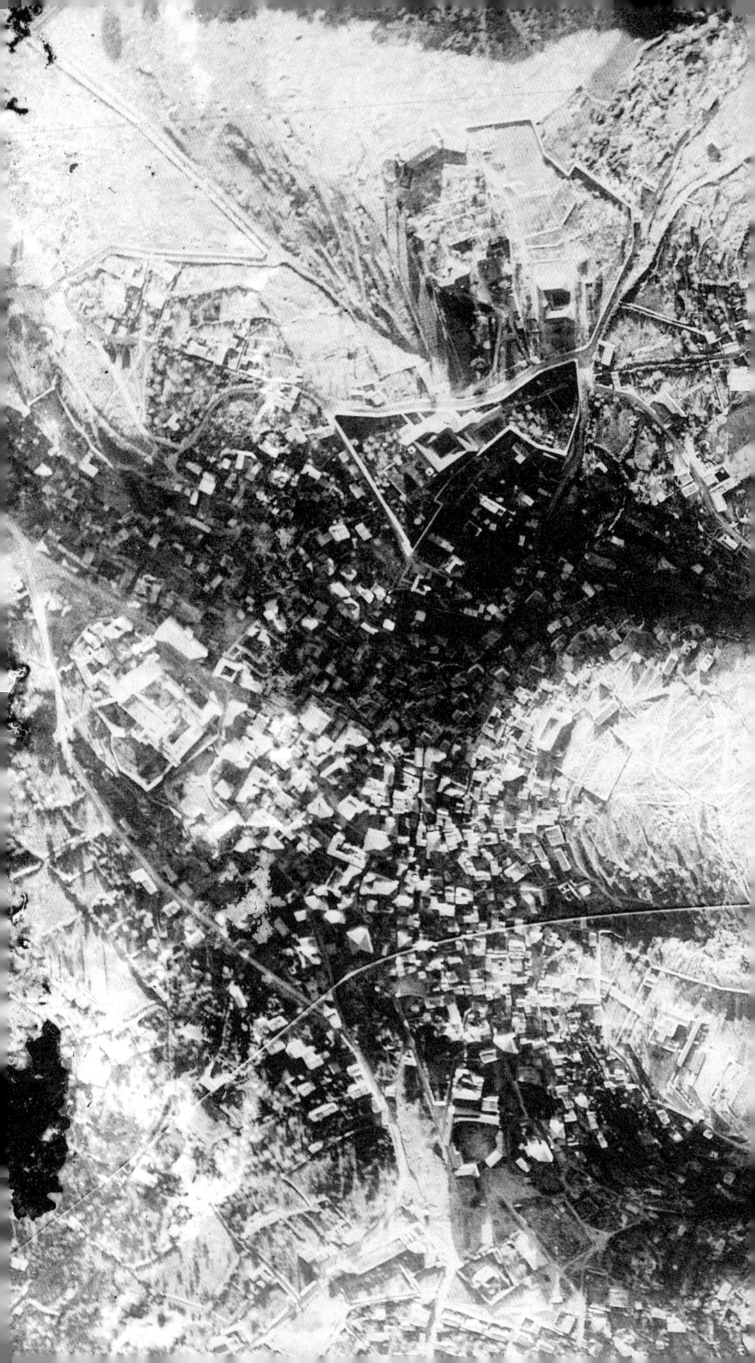

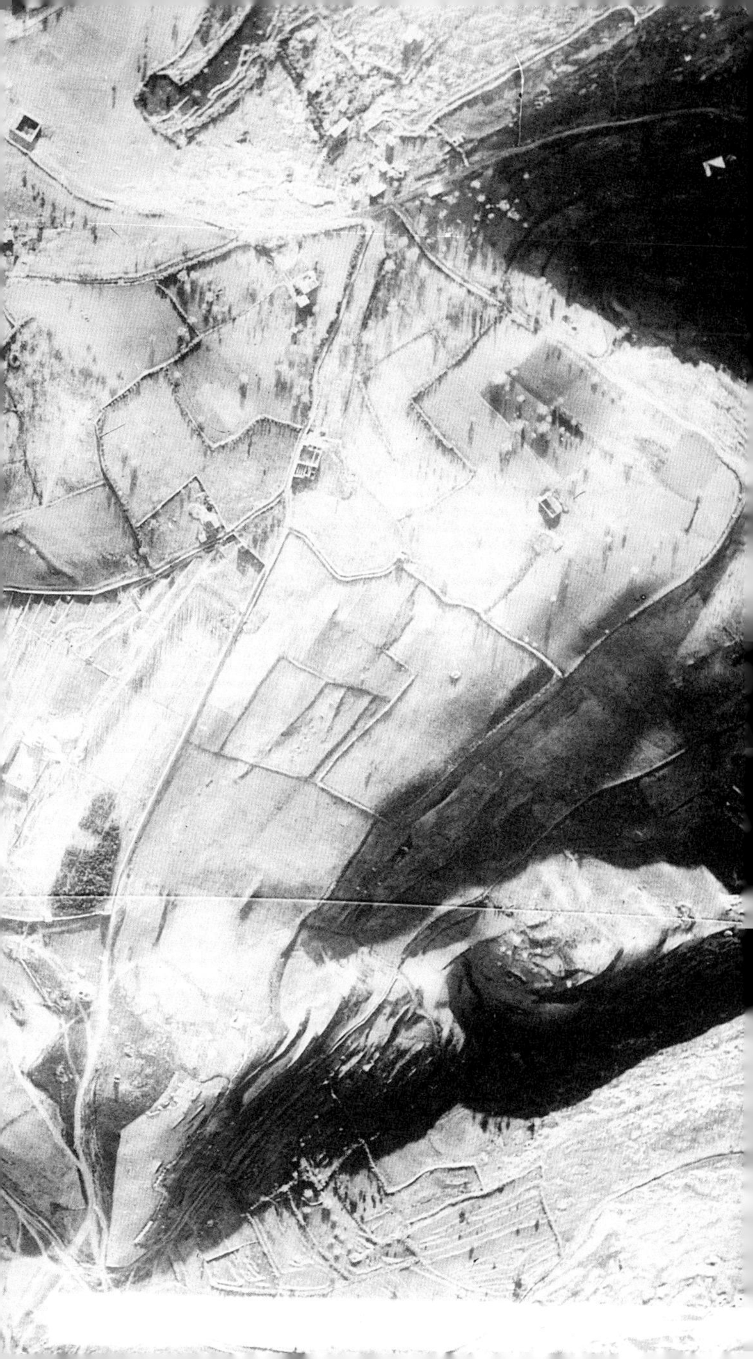

TIME
@TIME

Follow

Egyptian police detain a migrating stork on charges of spying | ti.me/18tpZky (via @TIMENewsFeed)

12:00 am - 2 Sep 2013

61 Retweets 17 Likes

18 61 17

Lord Blood @drng · 2 Sep 2013
Replying to @TIME
MT @TIME: Egyptian police detain a migrating stork on charges of spying ti.me/18tpZky
cc @aptronym @colvinius

1

aptronym ® @aptronym · 2 Sep 2013
@drng Talk about getting into a flap about nothing. @Colvinius

1 1

Lord Blood @drng · 2 Sep 2013
@aptronym @Colvinius I reckon they could keep holding the bird though on storking charges

1 1

aptronym ® @aptronym · 2 Sep 2013
@drng @Colvinius They've already got egg on their faces.

1

Lord Blood @drng · 2 Sep 2013
@aptronym @Colvinius arresting the pigeon was just jumping the shark

Erika is cautiously optimistic @Scimommy · 2 Sep 2013
Replying to @TIME
Did @TheOnion take over Time mag? "@TIME: Egyptian police detain a migrating stork on charges of spying | ti.me/18tpZky"

Angi Ali @_AngiAli · 2 Sep 2013
Replying to @TIME
OMG LOL!!!

"@TIME: Egyptian police detain a migrating stork on charges of spying | ti.me/18tpZky (via @TIMENewsFeed)"

Nature Conservation Egypt (NCE)
Page Liked · September 1, 2013 ·

NCE Statement | Re: #SPYDUCK (White Stork)
بيان الجمعية المصرية لحماية الطبيعة حول طائر اللقلق المضبوط بقنا

On Saturday, August 31st, news surfaced over the capture of a White Stork in Qena, referred to over social media as #SpyDuck, after concerned citizens suspected the stork was a tool of espionage because of the satellite tracking device attached to its back. Security apparatuses have already declared that this device poses no threat to Egypt's security, and a report is to be produced by a governmental veterinary committee.

Nature Conservation Egypt (NCE) has been contacted by the concerned Hungarian researchers responsible for tagging the "detained" White Stork, and they have provided (the already public) information on the specific stork in question.

Here is the captured stork's profile:
http://www.satellitetracking.eu/inds/view/111

And here is the satellite imagery of the captured stork's migration route:
http://www.satellitetracking.eu/inds/showmap/?check_111=111

Satellite tagging of birds is an internationally acknowledged practice used by researchers and conservationists to study the migration routes of birds. These results are then commonly used to influence local policies, to ensure the protection of migratory birds, particularly soaring birds, during their migration from north to south in Autumn, and south to north in Spring.

NCE is currently following up with the different administrative entities in Egypt to ensure that the necessary steps are taken for the release of this White Stork.

إنتشرت الأخبار بالأمس حول "إلقاء القبض" على طائر اللقلق بمحافظة قنا وذلك لحمل الطائر جهاز تتبع يستخدم لإجراء الأبحاث العلمية حول مسارات الهجرة للطيور.

أعلن مدير أمن قنا أن الطائر لا يحمل أي متفجرات أو أجهزة تجسس، ولكنهم منتظرين صدور تقرير من لجنة الطب البيطري.

تواصلت الجمعية المصرية لحماية الطبيعة مع الباحثين من دولة المجر المسئولين عن متابعة طائر اللقلق المحتجز، وقاموا بتوفير لنا العديد من الروابط المتعلقة بمتابعة الطائر المضبوط.

لمعرفة بيانات طائر اللقلق المضبوط:
http://t.co/4BLGvCiNj9

لمشاهدة مسار هجرة طائر اللقلق المضبوط ومعرفة أهمية تتبع الطيور المهاجرة، برجاء زيارة هذا الموقع الذي يوفر خريطة هجرته من أوروبا إلى أفريقيا:
http://t.co/WM5rFJNU5G

وجب علينا ملاحظة أهمية تلك الأبحاث العلمية حول مسارات هجرة الطيور المحتلفة, تلك الأبحاث تستخدم لتنفيذ إجراءات صون الطيور المهاجرة في الدول المختلفة ومنها مصر.

Arrested 'spy' stork killed and eaten after release in Egypt

Eyes on storks? Egyptian fisherman thought bird was foreign spy

Fowl play? Stork suspected of spying in Egypt was 'killed and eaten' by villagers

Stork Detained for Spying in Egypt

Arrested 'spy' stork found dead in Egypt

Stork 'jailed' in Egypt after spy accusation

'Spy' stork becomes dinner in Egypt

Suspected Egyptian Spy Stork Freed, Then Promptly Killed and Eaten

Egypt's 'spy stork' killed and eaten by villagers

Mistaken 'spy' stork released into wild

•• إطلاق سراح "الطائر الجاسوس" بعد غد.. ووفد من حقوق الحيوان يزوره في محبسه

From: **Halmos Gergő**
Date: Sun, Sep 1, 2013 at 11:14 AM
Subject: white stork with satellite tracking device in Qena

Dear Noor

We have found out from the media, that a white stork with our satellite tracking device was caught in Egypt near Qena and it is in captivity: http://www.dailymail.co.uk/news/article-2407948/Bird-thats-ruffling-government-feathers-Stork-suspected-SPY-detained-police-Egypt.html

Could you get in touch with the authorities and inform them, that this is a stork from Hungary and the device is a wildlife tracking device we attached to it to follow the migration of the bird. You can give my contact details If they need more information to release the bird. They can call or e-mail me. Or alternatively if you can find out contact details of those who keep the bird in captivity I can call them.

Even you can find the details of the bird and the tracking data on our satellite tracking website.

The route: http://www.satellitetracking.eu/inds/showmap/?check_111=111

The bird: http://www.satellitetracking.eu/inds/view/111

Thank you for your help in advance.

Gergő

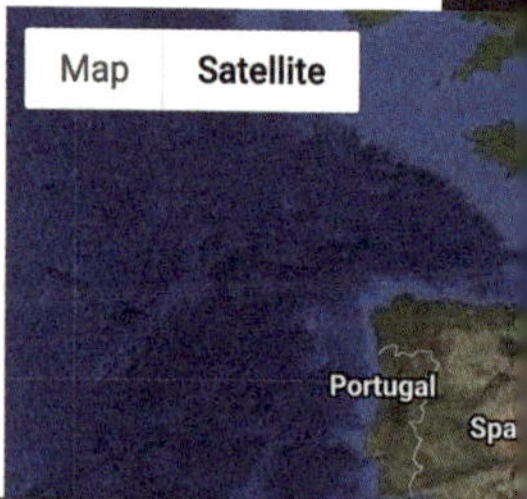

THE
ORNITHOLOGICAL SOCIETY
OF EGYPT

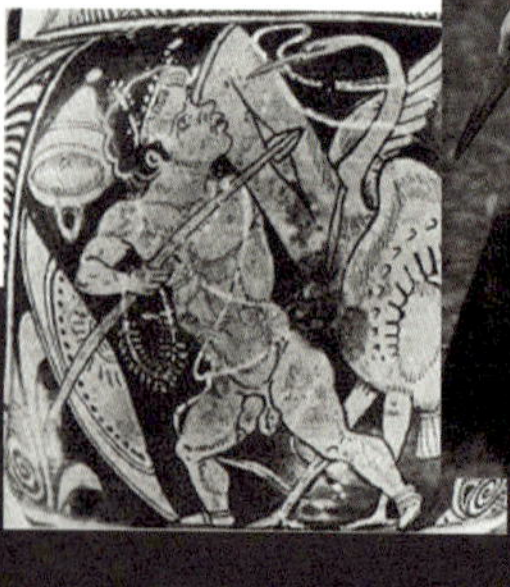

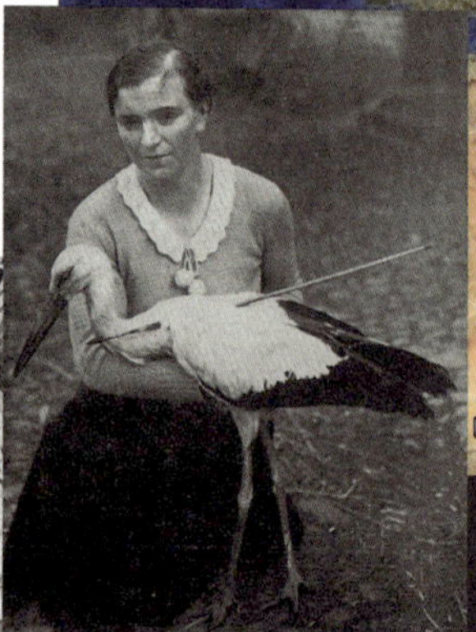

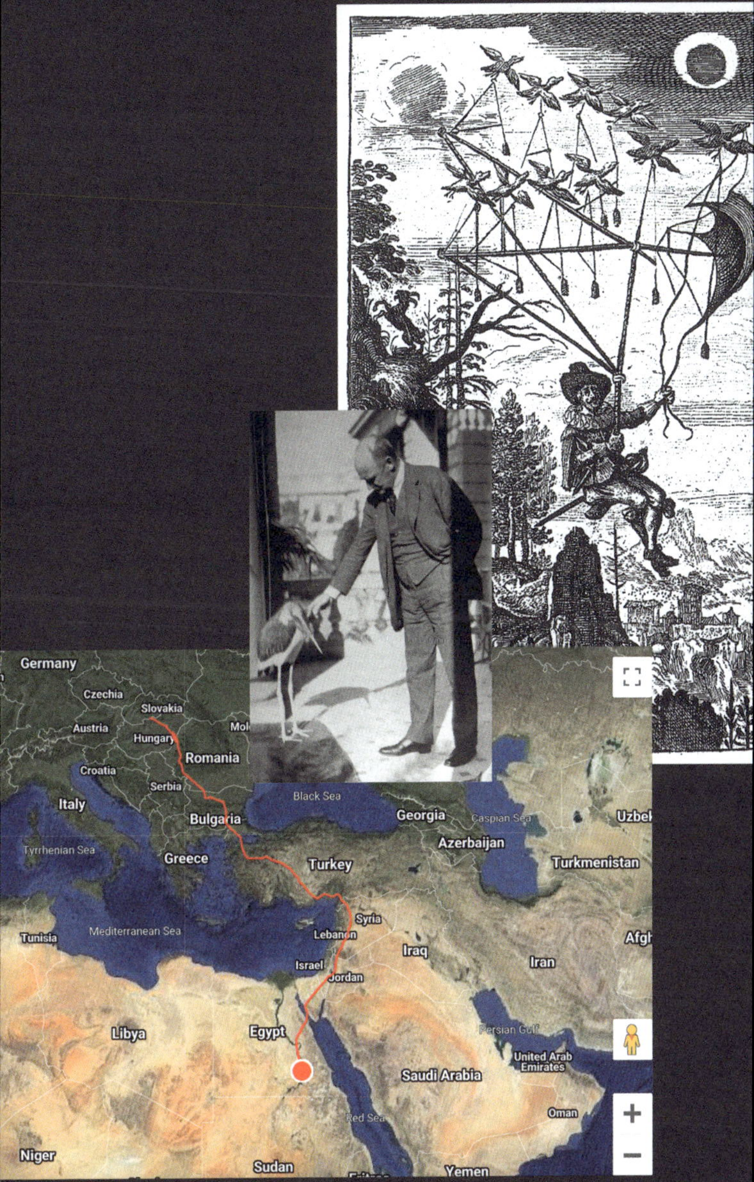
Germany
Czechia
Slovakia
Austria
Hungary
Romania
Croatia
Serbia
Italy
Bulgaria
Black Sea
Georgia
Caspian Sea
Azerbaijan
Tyrrhenian Sea
Greece
Turkey
Turkmenistan
Syria
Tunisia
Mediterranean Sea
Lebanon
Iraq
Iran
Israel
Jordan
Libya
Egypt
Persian Gulf
United Arab Emirates
Saudi Arabia
Red Sea
Oman
Niger
Sudan
Yemen

In 1822, a stork, known as the Rostocker Pfeilstorch, survived an attack in Central Africa and flew to Germany with an iron-tipped wooden spear in its neck. The unfortunate bird was then discovered and shot by a hunter in the town of Klütz, Mecklenburg-Vorpommern.

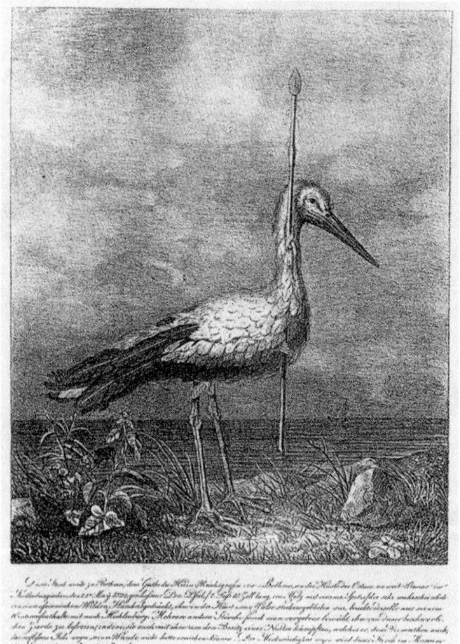

European storks that were injured by an arrow while spending winter in Africa—called *Pfeilstorch* ("arrow stork")—were crucial in understanding bird migration. Prior to this discovery, theorists had thought that during colder seasons birds flew to the moon or, as Aristotle believed, hibernated or mutated into other species.

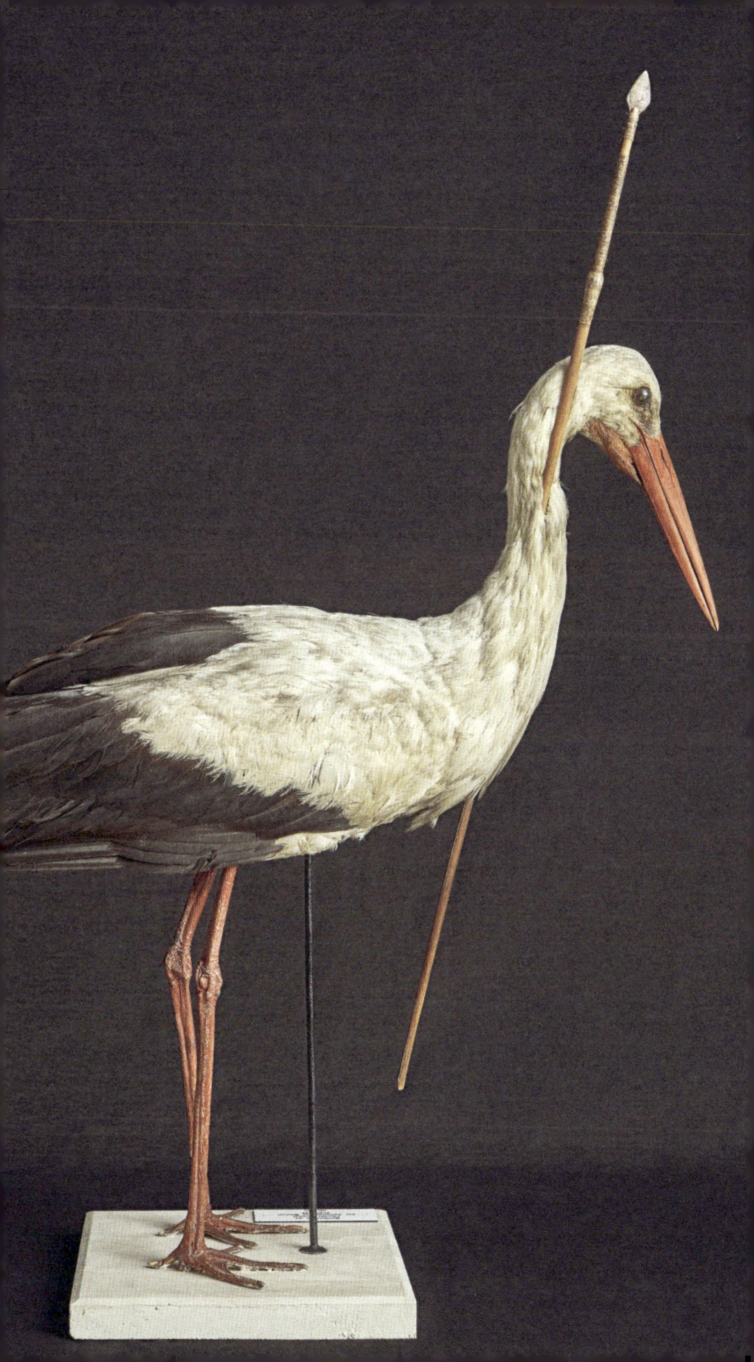

A Bird's-Eye View: The Release of Menes the Stork

Haitham Mossad

I work at the Wadi Allaqi Biosphere Reserve along the border of Egypt and Sudan. One afternoon, I received a phone call from Nature Conservation Egypt (NCE). I was told they had received a message from a researcher in Europe who was tracking migratory birds, but one of his monitored white storks, called Menes, seemed to be stuck in the city of Qena. NCE also told me that the media had reported a story about a stork—it was accused of espionage and had been taken into police custody.

I told all of this to my boss, and together we agreed that an official intervention was required because police and a jailed spy-bird were involved. Our office in Aswan is about three hundred kilometers from Qena, but we had connections to an environmental agency that put us in direct contact with the police station. We talked to the officer in charge and relayed the urgency of releasing the detained "spy." Obviously, the bird was not a spy, but the officers were afraid to take action in case he was some kind of threat. They needed someone else to take responsibility.

People don't typically capture storks in Qena, but the local children like to hunt birds for sport, rather than for food. The boy who caught the stork, however, brought him to his father who then took the bird to the police station. The father saw the tracking device on the bird's body—he imagined it could be an explosive or spying device and got scared.

The following morning, I packed posters, brochures, and booklets about the nature reserve in the car and embarked on my journey. I needed to convince the police officers and locals that it was important to inform their children about birds; it was an educational opportunity, I thought. The officer and his colleagues were awaiting my arrival to see what I was about, and why we cared so much about a bird. I sat at his desk, explained about my work that I am paid to do, and I told him that I had traveled all this distance in a government car, paid for by the people and their taxes. (In Egypt, it feels like one has to always relay the seriousness of his or her work and status by emphasizing credentials.) I talked about my education and travels to try to impress the officer. In the middle of our meeting, another officer entered the room with a detainee. "Treat him well," his boss told him, "even the bird has someone coming for him."

Even though there was a lot of bureaucratic paperwork to fill out, the procedure was finished quite quickly. While I waited to receive Menes, I met the vet who was taking care of him during his detainment. The poor bird had been in jail for two or three days by then. The vet expressed pride in his role keeping Menes healthy. He felt he was doing something important, something different. You see, this was a new idea to the vet. It was as if he was seeking my approval, and I confirmed that, indeed, his help was very important. He was a young guy, probably in his early twenties.

Before I even arrived for my meeting with the police, the media had already broadcast the story, which was accompanied by an image of the stork in jail. In some places in Egypt, people call the stork the "Iraqi duck." And so the comedy of the spy duck unfolded. The famous actor Ahmed Mekky even wrote the story into his TV series *El Kabeer Awy* about foreigners who came to save a spy bird.

The police officer was desperate to explain why the stork was put behind bars in the first place. He knew the media had turned them into a laughing stock. Apparently the station was far too crowded, so they decided that the safest place for Menes was in a cell.

He told me, "Look, he was making a mess in the entrance of the station. I want people to understand why I did this; it wasn't to reprimand the bird. The jail cell was the most convenient option." At one point, the bird was tied to a chair, but was frantic and flying everywhere. There was a ceiling fan in the office, he told me, and they were afraid it would harm him.

The officer wanted to be certain that I knew what I was getting myself in to, and that I was now taking responsibility for the bird. I responded with certainty and authority that, indeed, I knew what I was doing. I didn't come for fun, after all—I came because I take my job seriously, and because I had full support of the office I work for.

I took the bird back to the same place he was captured, but I didn't expect hundreds of people to come along to witness his release. Menes refused to fly. He just stood there. And everyone stood watching too. I picked him up and he didn't even fight. I tried to release him elsewhere, without people watching, but he still refused to fly. It was already getting late and I didn't want to leave him behind. By that point I was already dedicated to his well-being.

I drove Menes to Aswan. Since we arrived late, he spent the night at my house, in the bathroom where he could play in the water. The following morning, I followed the organization's usual protocol and took him to a holding cage in the first cataract, a protected island on the Nile. This is a rehabilitation unit for injured birds until they are ready for release. The security guy let him out every once in a while, and Menes would walk around the cage and then go back in. Then, the next day, he finally took off with another flock of migratory birds. I relayed the beautiful news to the team of scientists in Hungary; their bird had finally been safely released. But unfortunately the excitement was premature. Menes only made it to the next island, which was 1.5 kilometers away. The research team received an email from a stranger who had found the device.

Young kids had hunted the bird, and afterward they took the device back with them to Aswan. They told me about a flock of storks at rest and that all flew away except one. It was Menes. Perhaps he got too accustomed to being around humans, or he was weak.

He was consumed that evening.

It was a sad ending. We sent the device back to Hungary, where the researchers tracking the bird were based, so it could be used again to track another, hopefully more fortunate, bird. That being said, NCE's tracking data is used to determine obstacles that birds face along their migratory path. Knowing the bird's cause of death helps with their future research. Often the details of a bird's disappearance remain unknown. So at least Menes provided that.

Pages 52–57: Photographs of Menes after he was caught and detained on suspicion of espionage and of his release by Haitham Mossad in September 2013.

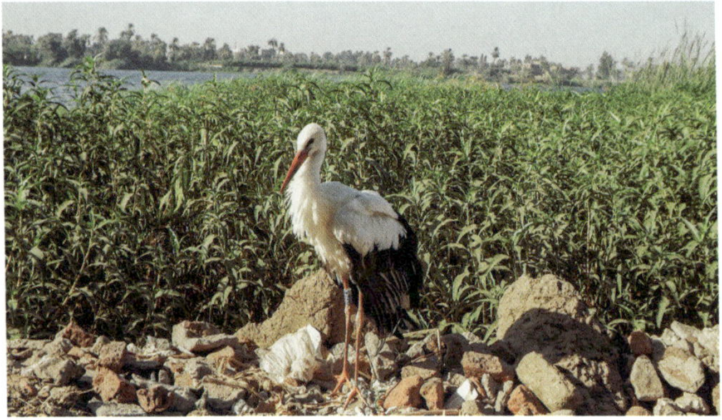

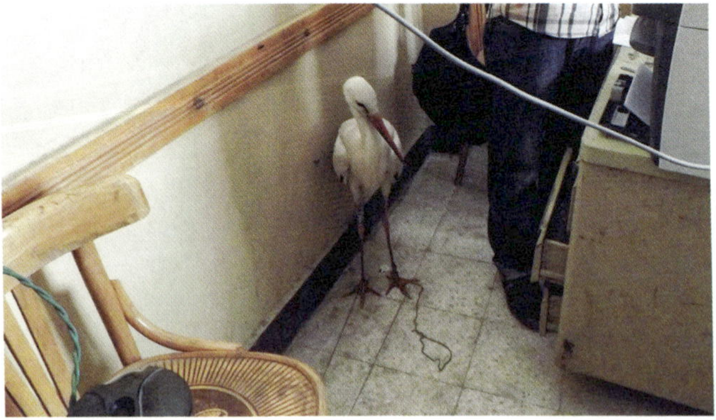

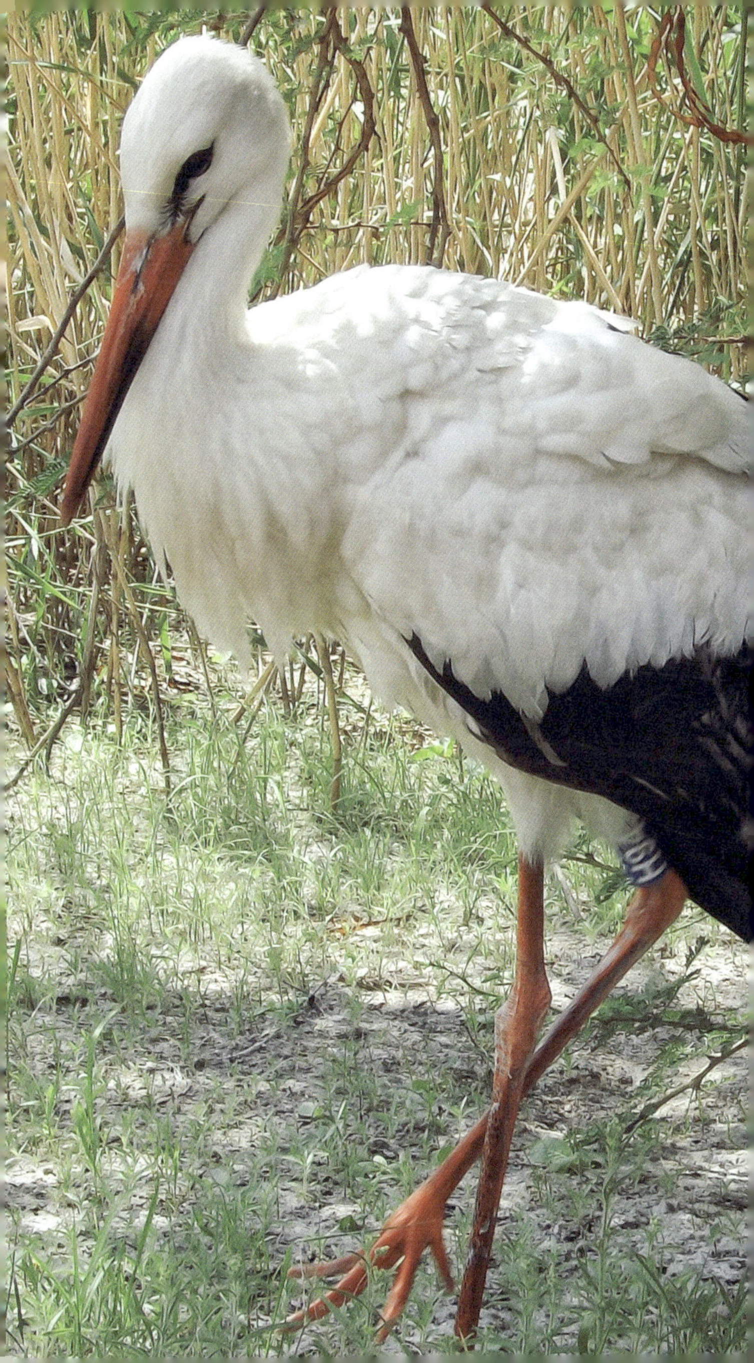

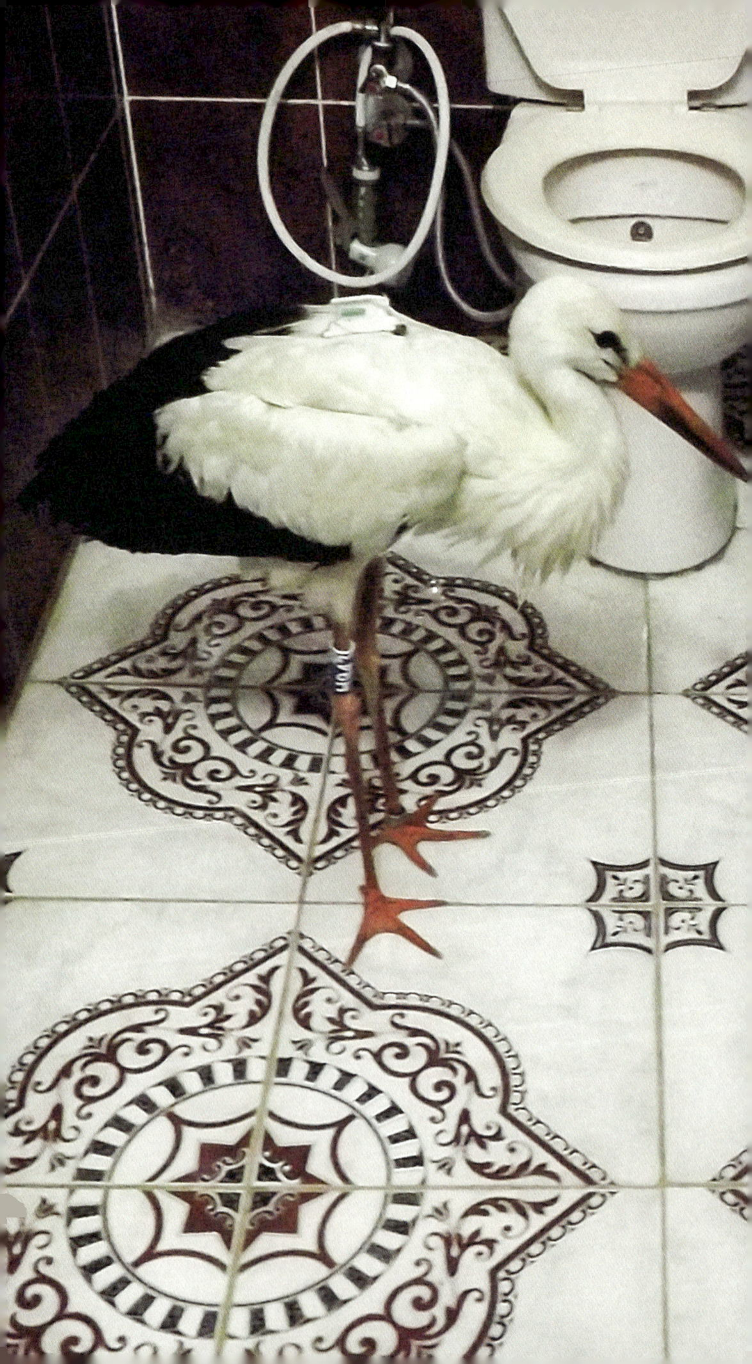

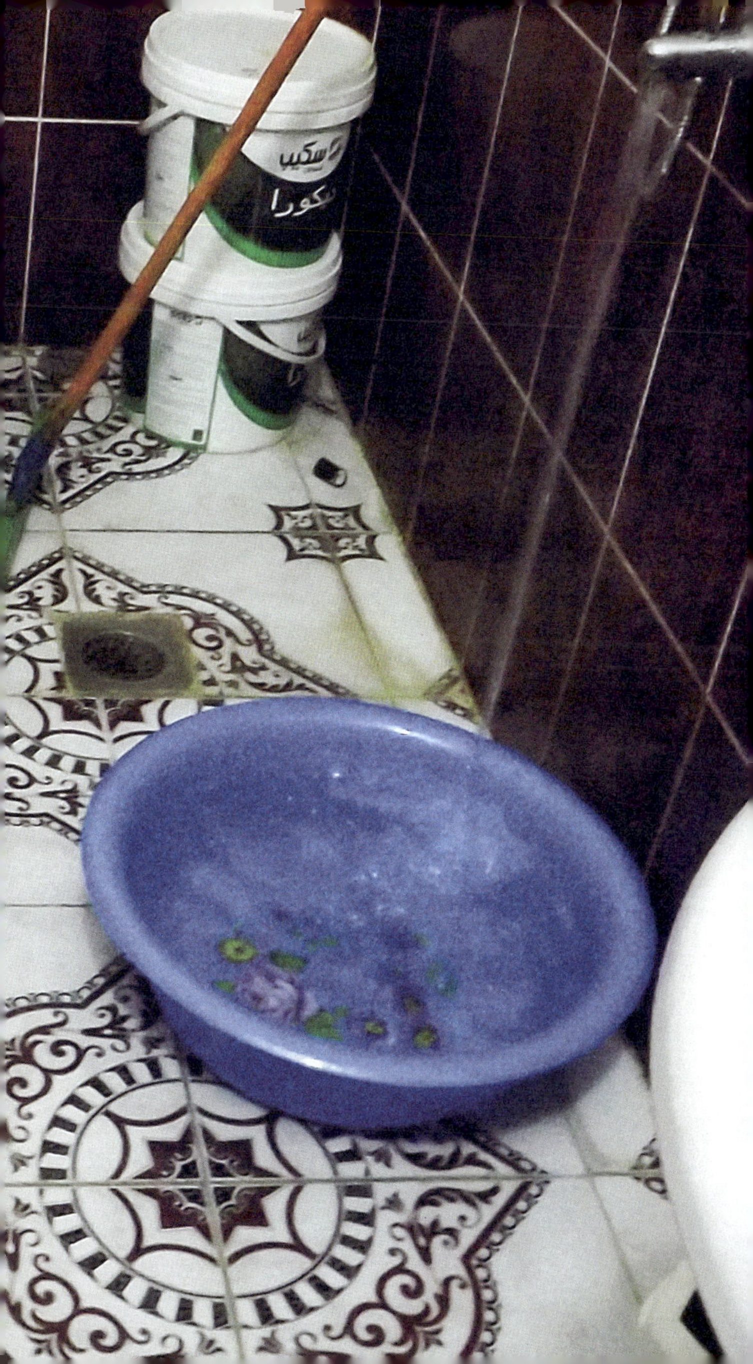
سكيب

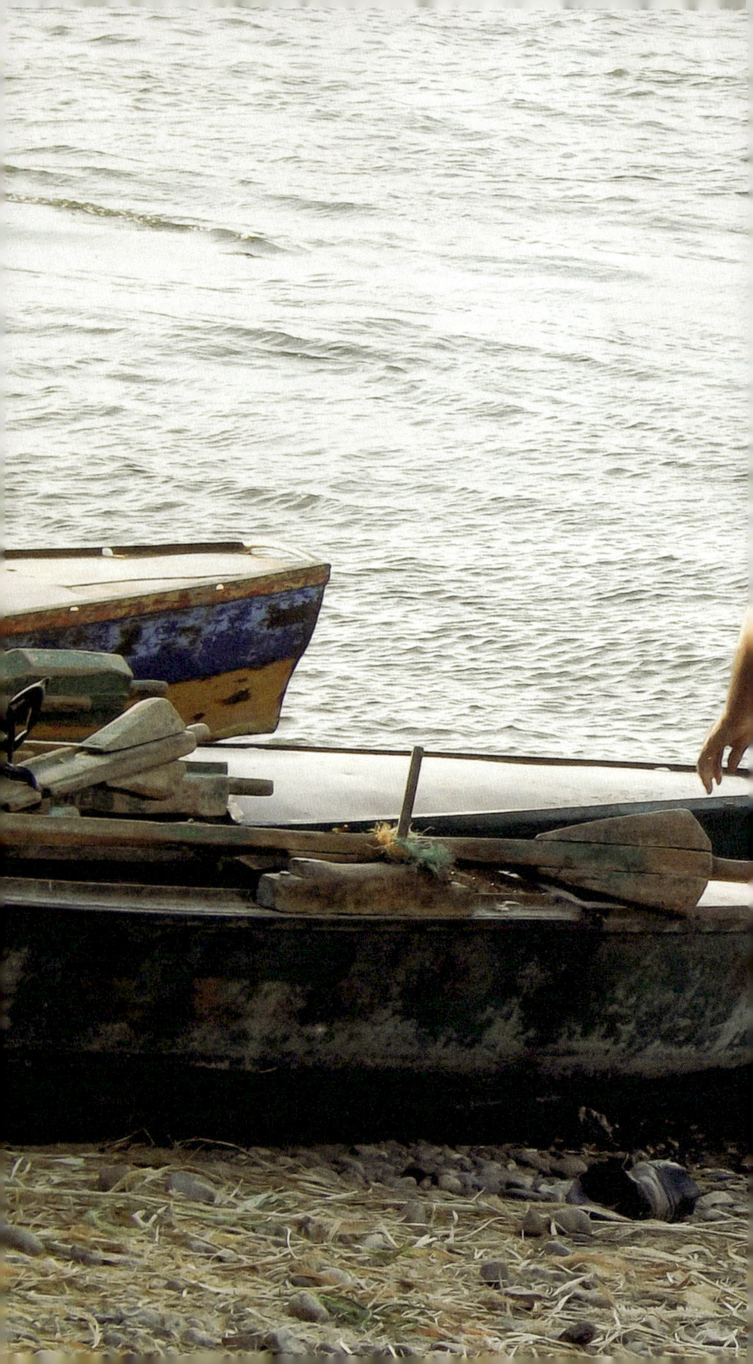

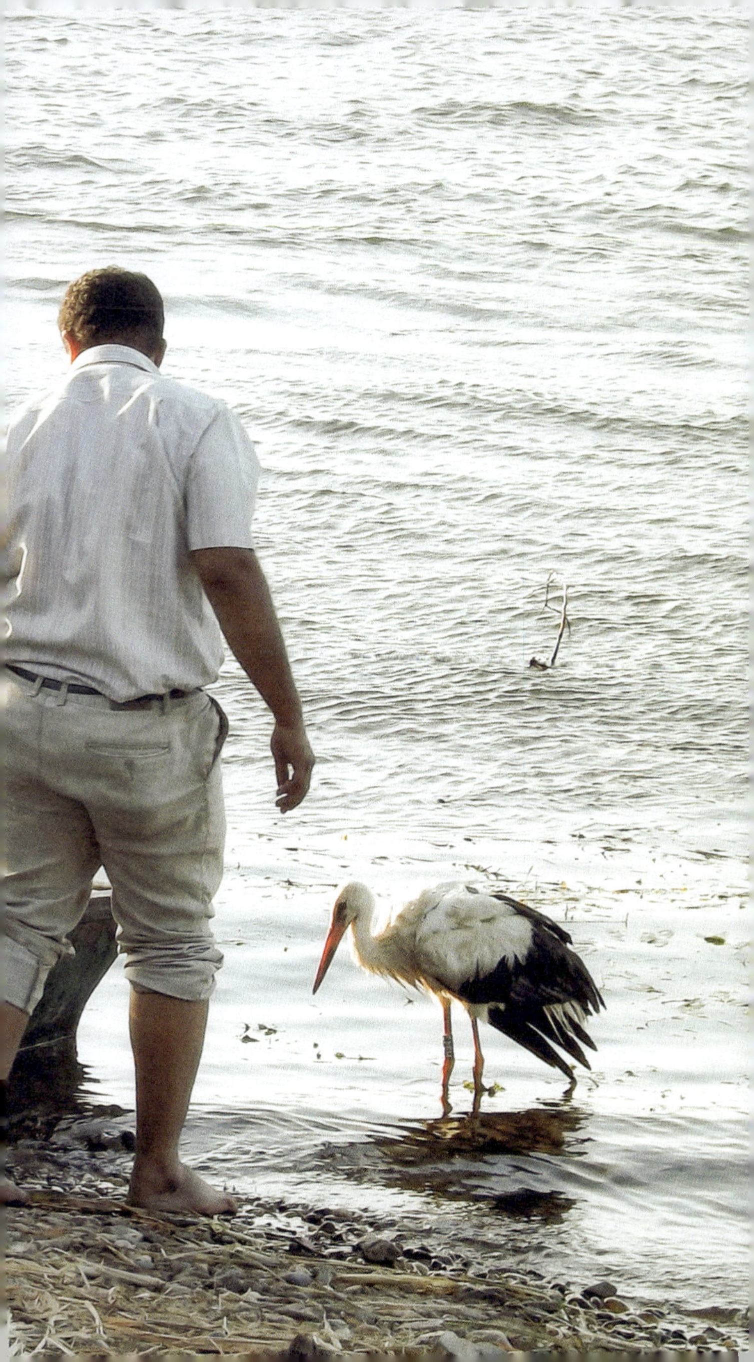

Reductio Ad Absurdum

Heba Y. Amin in conversation with Adel Iskandar

Heba Y. Amin The story of the spy stork went viral in 2013. How would you describe the Egyptian media that year under the rise and fall of Mohamed Morsi and the Muslim Brotherhood?

Adel Iskandar The most complicated period for the media in contemporary Egyptian history was from 2012 to 2013. The aftermath of the uprising in 2011 saw a dramatic and sudden deregulation of the media sector. Owing to pressure from the protest movement, the state institutions began to crumble: they lost control over public discourse, and the power over broadcast television, radio, and newspapers started to disintegrate. Furthermore, there was a significant populist pushback against most of those instruments of the state. We started to see a huge proliferation of new television and satellite stations being registered. The Egyptian Radio and Television Union (ERTU)—which is responsible for registering television satellite stations—began to sign off on as many stations as possible in an attempt to appease the popular disgruntlement. During the eighteen days of protest against Hosni Mubarak's government, the media was discredited to such an extent that a dramatic change was necessary. There were about twenty-six new satellite stations, and the number of newspapers getting licenses to print was remarkable (we're talking about twenty to thirty additional newspapers in six months). There was an incredible thirst for information, even in terms of online subscriptions and access to internet—everything was growing exponentially because people were curious and interested, compelled in conversations about politics and the future of their country.

A period of remarkable openness as far as what could and could not be discussed occurred in 2011/12; taboos were being shattered. There was talk about military rule, the various factions among Islamist groups and parties, and widespread political liberalization as well. Difficult issues were on the table—from women's rights to whether Islam should be a source of legislation in the country, and everything in between. The media liberalization was coupled with broader forms of social and political liberalization. There was a wide spectrum of political expression, from the revolutionary socialists, leftist parties, and openly communist groups to the emergence of Salafis, Islamists, and once-jihadist groups like the Hizb al-Bina wa al-Tanmiya (Building and Development Party). All of this was happening simultaneously, and each of these political groups began to utilize the media, with many launching their own media outlets or printing their own newspapers or running official and informal Facebook pages. For instance, the Muslim Brotherhood went from being a barely tolerated political group with scarce media presence to running a newspaper and a satellite television network in a span of one year. The Salafis also set up several television networks, and even the youth movement that led the 2011 revolution began broadcasting their own television station called January 25. This was coupled with a highly charged and engaged political environment characterized by near constant mobilization in the streets and frequent voting and balloting. This is the media and political context that frames the period before the spy-stork incident.

HYA What happened then?

AI The Muslim Brotherhood came to power in 2012. Mohamed Morsi was in the presidency for almost a year before another massive protest movement was initiated against him, the apex of which was June 30, 2013. As soon as the Muslim Brotherhood and Morsi were deposed from power, a few months before the spy stork and all the mayhem and ridiculousness around it happened in September, a complete shutdown of the media space that had opened up the year prior occurred. The case made by the state and all of its instruments—as well as the various allied political forces that agreed on the removal of Morsi from office—was that the media environment needed to change. The start of that change was the shutting down of the Muslim Brotherhood station Misr 25, the storming of the Al Jazeera offices by security forces, and the elimination of numerous newspapers affiliated with Islamist groups. Basically, anyone who was out of line with this new message—concerning the end of Muslim Brotherhood rule—and the return to another road map shepherded by the military was going to become a target. And this was happening with a substantial amount of popular support and fanfare. As everything began to shut down, discussion regarding the prohibition of certain political groups, such as the Muslim Brotherhood, began to be heard.

In the months that followed, an organized protest movement, which took place at two sites—at Rabaa al-Adaweya Square and al-Nahda Square—became the epicenter of the anti-military and anti-coup movements with an Islamist agenda that supported the return of Morsi to the presidential palace. Between July 4, 2013—when the Muslim Brotherhood was physically removed from office—and August 14—when pro-Morsi sit-ins were violently dispersed—the country was in a state of *taabe'a* (which literally means "to fill" but has been used politically to suggest mobilizing, or to "hunker down," or to suggest preparations for hardship and confrontation). This expression resonates throughout Egyptian political history including periods ahead of wars or in the run up to important political moments. During this delicate period in the summer of 2013, rallies continued throughout the country signaling an impending collision between the state and all of its supporters on one side, and the Muslim Brotherhood and the anti-coup movement on the other. This came to a head on August 14 when the pro-Morsi and Muslim Brotherhood protest campsites in Rabaa and Nahda squares were forcibly and brutally dispersed by armed security forces and people were massacred; this marked the end point. After that there was no more protesting, and no more Muslim Brotherhood. The organization was subsequently banned and designated as a terrorist group. At the time, the government was still not entirely militarized, but it was apparent that the military was rapidly becoming the go-to source for information and the de facto power in the country. The military as now presented as a heroic institution because it "saved" Egypt from the Muslim Brotherhood's rule (unless you were a Brotherhood supporter).

When the stork made headlines, Egypt was extremely charged and deeply divided, violence was rampant, and the state was launching a full-frontal attack against its pro-Morsi opposition. This was a period of tremendous suspicion toward anybody who disapproved or was critical of the government. Everyone was a potential adversary or potential culprit, and the Muslim Brotherhood became this nebulous thing where nobody knew who did or didn't supported it. There was a growing paranoia, the state actively manufactured fear and loathing of various opposition groups, there was a "you're with us or against us" mentality, and a war-on-terror attitude, similar to what exists in the United States and other parts of Western Europe. The Egyptian brand, however, was on steroids.

HYA But wasn't there also skepticism toward outside influences as well, rather than just internal players?

AI Exactly. There was so much suspicion about outside forces and who's supporting whom: fear of Qatar, the Turks, and anyone who openly supported the Muslim Brotherhood, coupled with the age-old suspicions of Israel and whether the Zionist state was somehow acting to undermine Egypt. It's very easy to bring Israel into the conversation whenever there's a period of fear and paranoia because many different generations have perceived Israel as an enemy owing to the Arab–Israeli wars of 1956, 1967, 1973, the multiple conflicts it has had with its neighbors, and the systematic dehumanization of Palestinians. For the past few decades, the idea that Israel is spying on Egypt has been hyped up by the media, whether it's through news programs or the entertainment industry. This was a very easy way to manufacture panic.

HYA Aside from the paranoia, which is quite easy to understand within that context you just explained, I was struck by the fact that the stork story was predominantly perpetuated by foreign media, rather than local outlets. The articles were ridiculous and circulated without any context. After listening to you, I wonder if some of the foreign media were using this story to critique the outcome and aftermath of the uprising and address the absurd turn that Egyptian politics took.

AI That's a really important point. One of the big problems facing foreign correspondence and reporting on the Middle East—and Egypt in particular—is that it is often driven by sensationalism. This also applies to coverage of sub-Saharan Africa, Southeast Asia, and places where Western media institutions tend not to invest time, energy, and personnel to cover the stories. Coverage is quick and fleeting. Geared to audiences in North America and Western Europe, an interesting and compelling story has a built-in absurdity to it. Either it's a story a reader can relate to or feel like they have something in common with those distant and foreign people or places, or it's an outrageously strange and eccentric story that becomes clickbait. We're living in a period when virality matters. A story about a stork that has been detained on accusations of espionage is not only interesting, but also telling about a political, social, and cultural time when nothing in Egypt is making sense to the outside world. A story of a spy stork perpetuates the existing narrativization of absurdity around Egypt. I think there is even a tendency to see Egypt as a place where strange and mystical things happen and people behave in illogical ways. I will go off on a limb here and say that, in fact, this is part of standard Western orientalization of Egypt that dates back to the mid-1800s. Lord Cromer, in the early 1900s, wrote his entire memoirs about what it means to govern Egypt. He described Egyptians as lacking in logical faculty and that the things that you cannot accept in Britain are standard practice in places like Egypt: you should expect the unexpected; everything is weird. If this is the way the Middle East has always been perceived by the West, then why couldn't a stork be a spy within such paradigms? But then there's another view that has to do with the way in which media is produced. Nowadays, context doesn't really matter in news, especially around 2013 when people were using little nuggets of information to turn them into stories. All it took then and now to build a story was a single tweet; there were entire stories built around a single tweet that would find their way on to the front page of the *New York Times*. A tweet consists of a maximum of 140 characters, and sometimes the story posted isn't fact-checked, especially when media organizations are competing over a scoop.[1] Of course, in 2013, there was an incredible thirst for information about Egypt. Interestingly, with the uprising in Egypt and the protests happening around the region, Cairo actually became a hub for foreign media programming and news production for the entire region between 2011 and 2013. If a journalist wanted to cover Libya, they came to Egypt; if they wanted to cover Bahrain, they came to Egypt. Then, when that door suddenly shut and there was no access to information, the story of the stork became the thread that any and all journalists were hanging on to. There was nothing else to report on. The story captured the imagination of the people, and it became like a feeding frenzy: you throw something into a bowl of piranhas and everyone is jumping around, trying to find out more. Before you know it, it doesn't matter whether or not there was a stork or if there was an arrest or anything of the sort.

HYA When I did some further research about Qena, where the bird was caught, I discovered that the city had a very complex political history, complete with a secret American military air base and an attempted rescue mission during the 1979 Iran hostage crisis in which fifty-two American diplomats and citizens were held hostage for 444 days (November 4, 1979–January 20, 1981) after a group of Iranian students—supporters of the Iranian revolution—took over the US Embassy. Operation Eagle Claw (April 24–25, 1980) was an attempt to rescue the Americans held hostage, but failed miserably and damaged US prestige worldwide in the process under President Jimmy Carter. Eight helicopters were sent from the military base in Qena, Egypt, and all encountered technical problems: one encountered hydraulic problems, another got caught in a cloud of fine sand, a third showed cracks in the rotor blade, and, lastly, one of the helicopters crashed into a transport aircraft killing eight servicemen and one Iranian citizen. This helped me better contextualize where the paranoia about the stork was coming from, in addition to the tension of events unfolding in the country in 2013.

In his text "Phantom Images," German filmmaker Harun Farocki critiques the aestheticized reflection of war and questions the normalization of military image technologies that later find their way into civilian life. He was particularly struck by the 1990/91 Gulf War, Operation Desert Storm, which exposed viewers to a new kind of image of military vision through the vantage point of the machine of destruction. This was the first time that images from cameras onboard US bombers were broadcast to television audiences, but we've since become more and more accustomed to the detached perspective of the bird's-eye view. We are talking about a bird with a migration device, so we can't ignore the embedded narrative of the bird's-eye view and how that perspective directly correlates with weapons of warfare. I wanted to connect this to your concept of "contextual objectivity" as a critique of media's coverage of war.

AI I'm really glad you mention Farocki's work because as someone who has lived through that period, the argument that he's making is extremely resonant. During the first Gulf War, we began to see the weaponization of the media, not just in an instrumental sense where it becomes a weapon, but in the fetishization of weaponry, technology, and innovation at the expense of real human stories. At that time, CNN was the first news channel to have 24/7 live coverage of the war, literally from above. Christiane Amanpour, Bernard Shaw, Peter Arnett, and others became the gold standard of television war coverage; they described the landscape of war at a safe distance from whatever was happening on the ground. For example, Arnett, who was the top correspondent from Baghdad, described their coverage in his memoir as a "bird's-eye view" of the whole event, but from the ninth floor of the Al-Rashid Hotel! The idea of the landscape of war means that minutia is less important; there was a fascination and obsession with the big picture and war could only be seen from a distance. The images of anti-aircraft fire over Baghdad and the green lights, for instance, became iconic. We were familiar with the aerial machinery of war—the F-14 Tomcats, F-16s, F-24s, AWACS, F-117A Nighthawk stealth bombers, B-52s, and so on (these names were drilled into our minds)—because those are the mediated main characters in the conflict, not the humans on the ground. And, ironically, they were also the ones bringing about "peace." We were watching these mechanical birds on TV as if they were the most important part of the war. News stories today show landscapes that are destroyed and people who are pulled out of the rubble, but in 1990/91 there were no Iraqis or Iraqi landscapes to be thought about, contemplated, lamented on, or mourned. The only Iraqi who existed on television was Saddam Hussein—and maybe his information minister, Mohammed Saeed al-Sahhaf—who was there to play the role of the absurd caricature, whose mere presence justified the bombardment. I use the phrase "contextual objectivity" to think through what it means for news organizations to challenge not only the status quo of programming, but to challenge their own expectations and decide whether or not there's a need to find another angle on the story. Let's assume that US news broadcasters are invested in covering a conflict that involves US military. Are they going to think about whether or not there are different contexts to be contemplated? Is objectivity a sum of all of these different contextual approaches, or does it mean to be devoid of opinion?

The journalistic mantra of "objectivity" is usually about avoiding opinion and partisanship and just presenting the facts, but actually that is probably the most problematic way to do news media and journalistic coverage. That's the kind of stuff that helped produce the so-called CNN effect in which the Gulf War was presented in the first place. They're saying: "I'm just describing the machinery, that's pretty objective. We're not advocating or cheerleading for the war, we're just describing it."

HYA It also relieves them of any accountability.

AI Absolutely. They come off scot-free because nobody can point fingers and say they are a part of the war or advocating it or sugarcoating it. What happens when you're not in the right place at the right time, or not where you belong, or not understanding that there are different locales in this conflict? It's like the idea of embedded journalism where reporters join a military regimen and that's their purview, angle, or lens through which they see the conflict. The camera is on one side of the conflict. The contextual objectivity argument is to say that if you are actually committed to objectivity, you should do away with this idea that you have to be positivist and distanced from human experience and instead get closer to human experience, with all of its colors, complexities, and nuances. Actually, contextual objectivity is about the constellation of different opinions that exist within the landscape of the story. A story has so many different angles that are impossible to even fathom. That is why covering Egypt between 2011 and 2013 was so complicated. There were nearly ninety million stories in the country in 2013—one for each Egyptian. How can you possibly translate that into meaningful coverage to the outside world? When journalism is committed to simplification, it produces information for the lowest common denominator. Not only then is nuance lost, but so too is commitment to context; context is the first to be discarded. All that is left are the so-called facts. Journalism just becomes mechanical and then nothing really makes sense.

HYA How do you think journalism has shifted, especially with citizen journalism? Where does that leave us today in terms of political expression?

AI One of the great things about the uprisings in the Middle East and elsewhere in the world is that there is an increasing democratization of the media. People who witness things or are part of a story are now able express their opinions and their perspectives through various platforms; they are being listened to. We are also witnessing a significant demise in mainstream programming and journalism. While CNN, Al Jazeera, BBC, and others are still the go-to networks for breaking news, they themselves can only legitimize their coverage on the basis of testimonies and anecdotes from the ground and from the people who are there. You'll notice that mainstream news organizations in operation today can't function without relaying messages and information posted by individuals on social media, and largely rely on the number of times a tweet is shared. There is a hefty reliance now on individual voices from these different places. Coverage ascertained and distributed from places like Syria, Libya, or Yemen, depends very heavily, if not completely, on local voices sending out this information. Today, you can't cover Yemen if you're a foreign correspondent. You simply cannot go there without facing considerable risks due to the ongoing conflict. Travel restrictions abound and foreign journalists are often seen as targets or bargaining chips for warring factions vying for power, influence, control, and material resources. Besides, few news organizations want to pay the insurance for the lives of journalists in a war zone. Instead they pay stringers and freelancers and locals who will risk their lives every day to get a story. While the feeling is that a more authentic perspective is given, in reality, we're still in a place where the structures of the institutions are largely the same since the 1990s, only the constellation of voices are much more voluminous and substantial. If you look at the frequency of loss of life, arrest, injury, prosecution, and other prices paid by local journalists covering stories for Western and international news agencies, it is truly astounding. So while citizen journalism is both more affordable and contextual than sending professional salaried foreign correspondents, it has come at a hefty cost to local reporters. We have yet to see the rise of another model in broadcasting, media production, and news content production that balances these inequities, values all lives equally, and produces sophisticated nuanced information from multiple perspectives.

1 In 2017, the text limit of a post on Twitter was increased from 140 to 280 characters.

Pages 72–73: A map showing the location of the Dandarah Temple complex in Egypt, a wall detail, and a photograph of the American military airbase in Wadi Qena (26.555058°N 33.132877°E). The airbase was used by the US Armed Forces as part of Operation Eagle Claw in 1980.

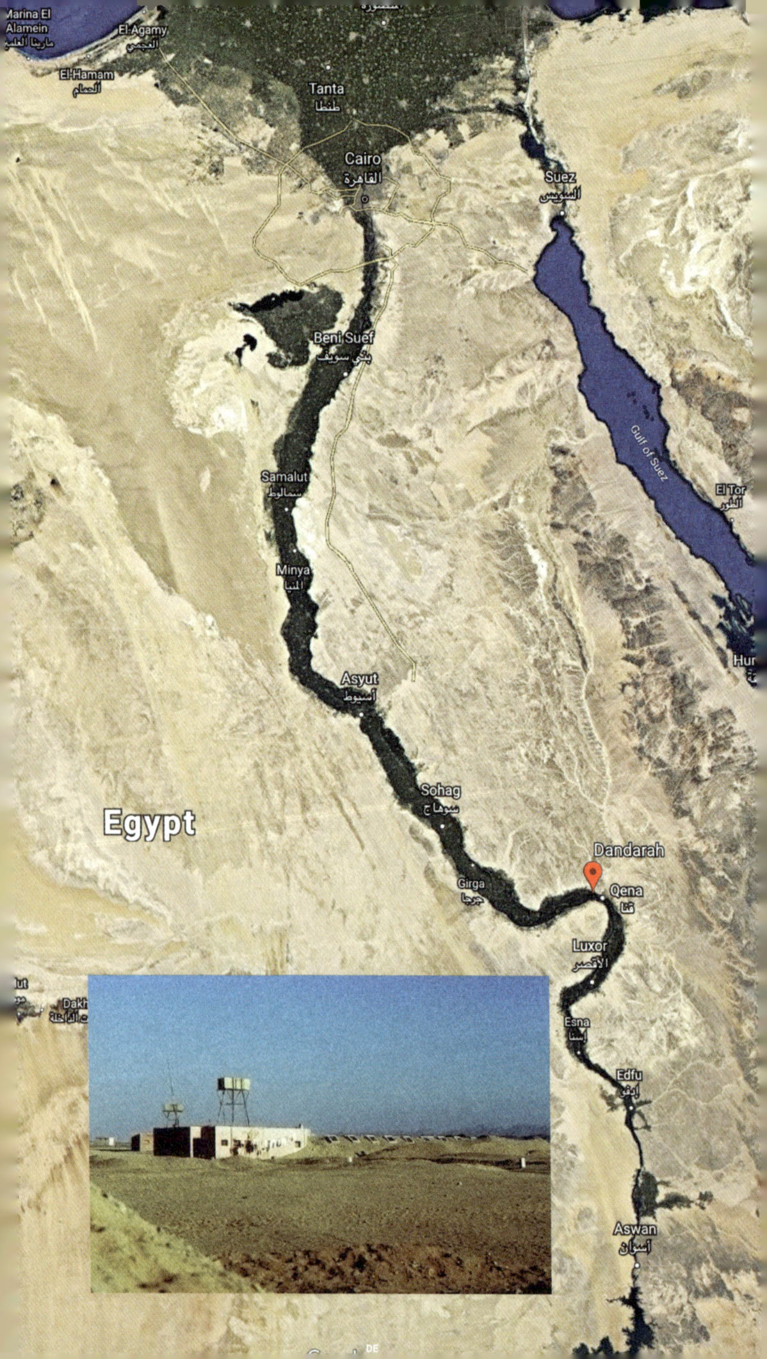
Marina El Alamein
El-Agamy
El-Hamam
Tanta
Cairo
Suez
Beni Suef
Gulf of Suez
El Tor
Samalut
Minya
Asyut
Sohag
Egypt
Dandarah
Qena
Girga
Luxor
Esna
Edfu
Aswan

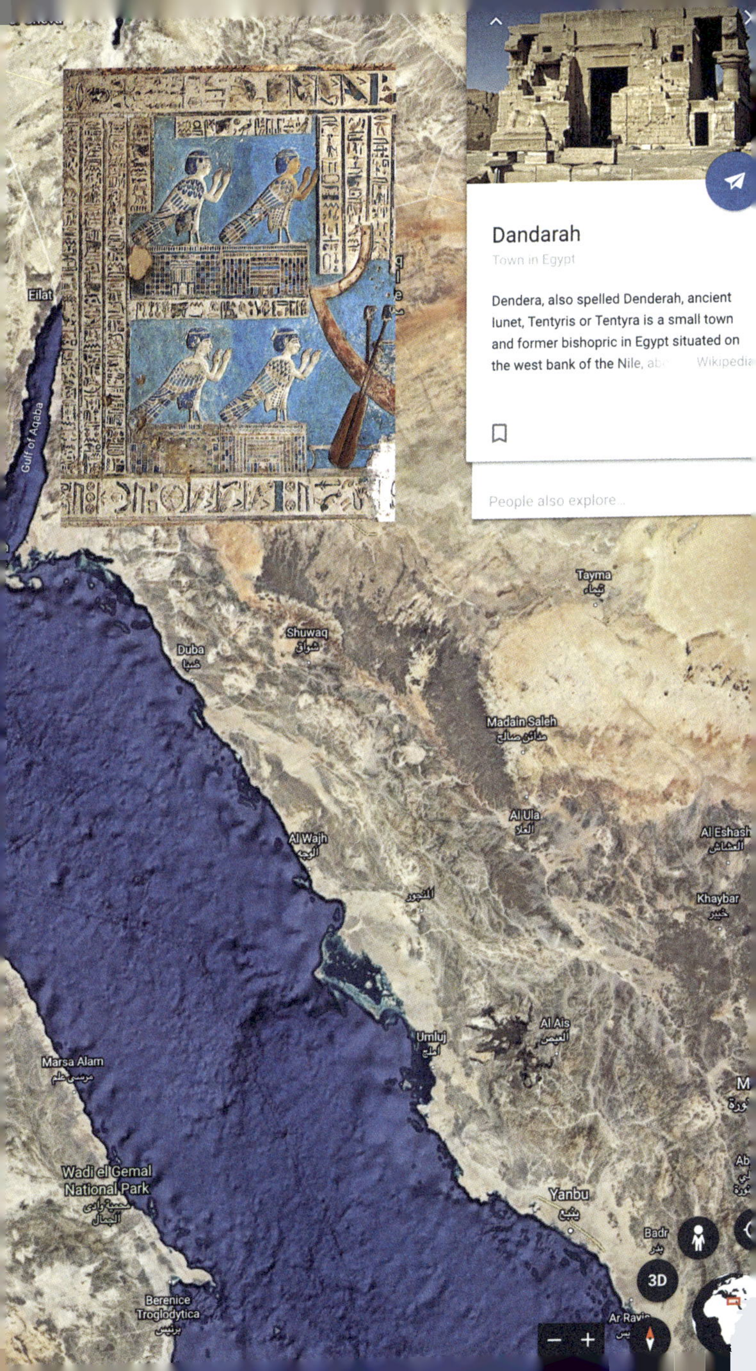

Dandarah
Town in Egypt
Dendera, also spelled Denderah, ancient Iunet, Tentyris or Tentyra is a small town and former bishopric in Egypt situated on the west bank of the Nile, ab
Wikipedia
People also explore...
Eilat
Gulf of Aqaba
Tayma
Shuwaq
Duba
Madain Saleh
Al Ula
Al Eshash
Al Wajh
Khaybar
Al Ais
Umluj
Marsa Alam
Wadi el Gemal National Park
Yanbu
Badr
3D
Berenice Troglodytica
Ar Rayis

The following is an account from Larry Grinnell, a US military technical communicator. Excerpt from www.larrygrinnell.com.

"The 1st Comm had an ongoing mission sending people to a classified location somewhere in the middle east, simply known to us as USAFE Forward Operating Location Alpha, or simply Site Alpha. As it turns out, this was the forward base that launched the rescue attempt to bring back the American hostages in Iran, taken when the US Embassy was invaded in 1979. The rescue attempt, Operation Eagle Claw, failed completely due to many factors that are probably still being discussed today. No one was supposed to know where [the base] was until they were under way, unless they had the appropriate clearances and need to know. [...] Gee, I thought, just having seen King Tut's riches, this was pretty amazing to be going to the country where he came from. We finally touched down, after going around three times due to difficult weather at the site, and when I got to the open doorway, my heart sunk. There it was. Miles and miles of miles and miles. This was a real desert with basically nothing.

I quickly found out that Site Alpha was a former Soviet air base, built in the days when the Soviets and the Egyptians were fast friends. [...] Officially it was known as Wadi Qena [...]. We called it Bum F**k Egypt (BFE for short). Along with Thule, Greenland and Minot, North Dakota, BFE was an often mythical place that military training instructors threatened to send you if you didn't get with the program. I think we even had a sign outside Base Operations that said 'Welcome to BFE,' but when local Egyptian military folks and civilian dignitaries visited, the true meaning of BFE was masked with the acronym 'Beautiful, Friendly Egypt.' I don't think anyone was fooled, but we did at least try to play the game."

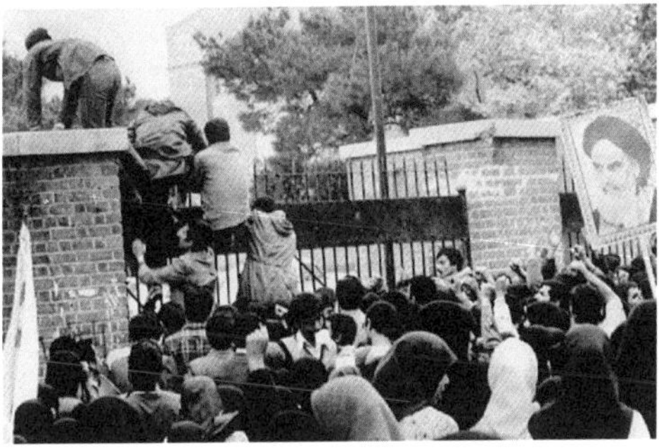

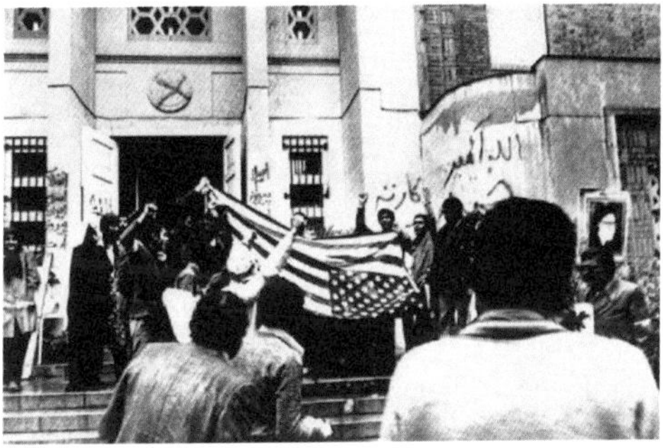

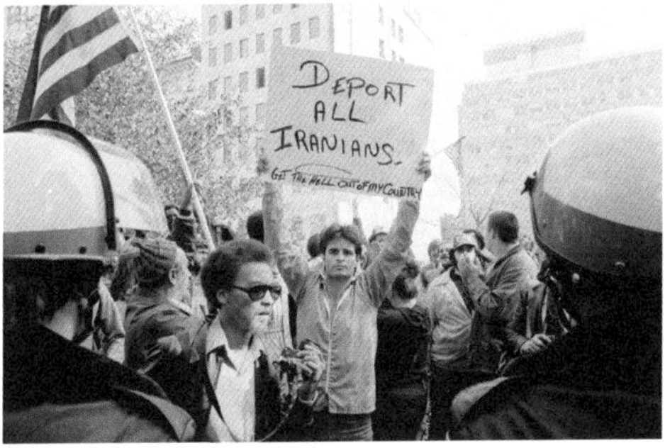

Photographs of the Iran Hostage Crisis: (*top* and *middle*) students storm the US Embassy in Tehran on November 4, 1979; (*bottom*) a man holds up a sign during a US protest in 1979.

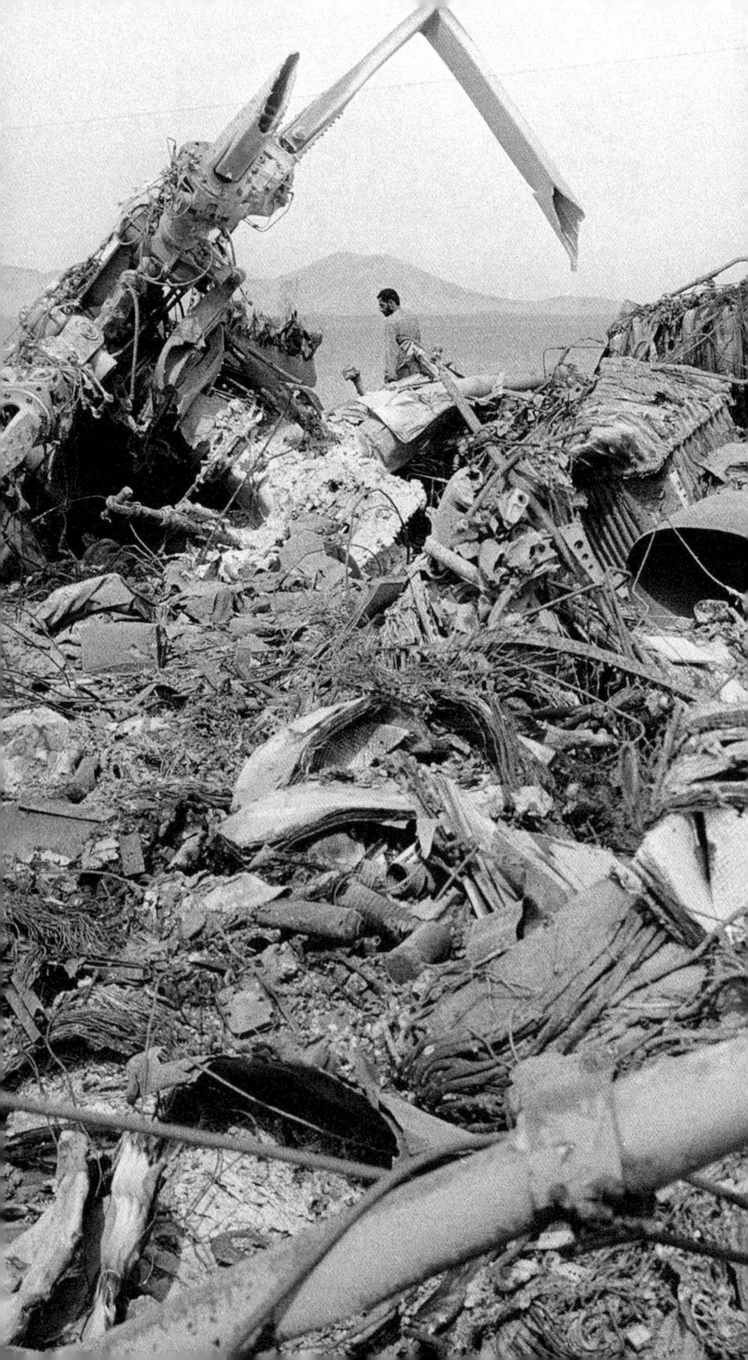

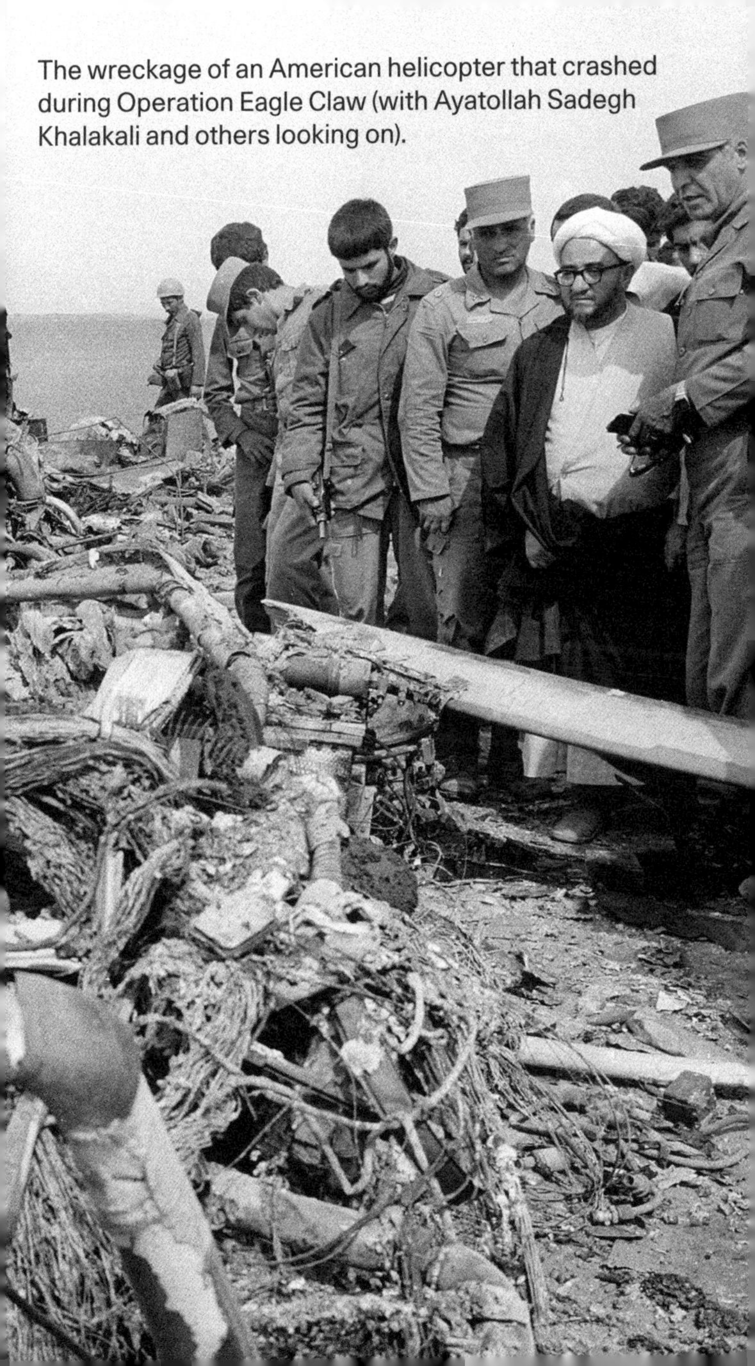

The wreckage of an American helicopter that crashed during Operation Eagle Claw (with Ayatollah Sadegh Khalakali and others looking on).

Patent drawing for a flying machine (US Patent #95513) filed to the Patent and Trademark Office by W. F. Quinby in 1869.

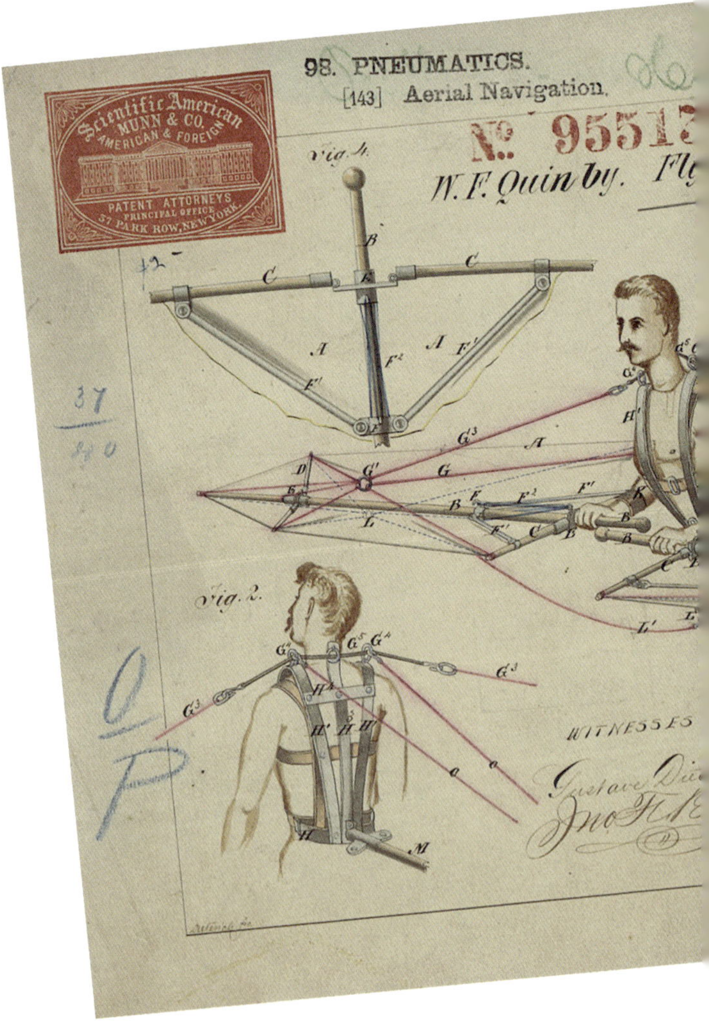

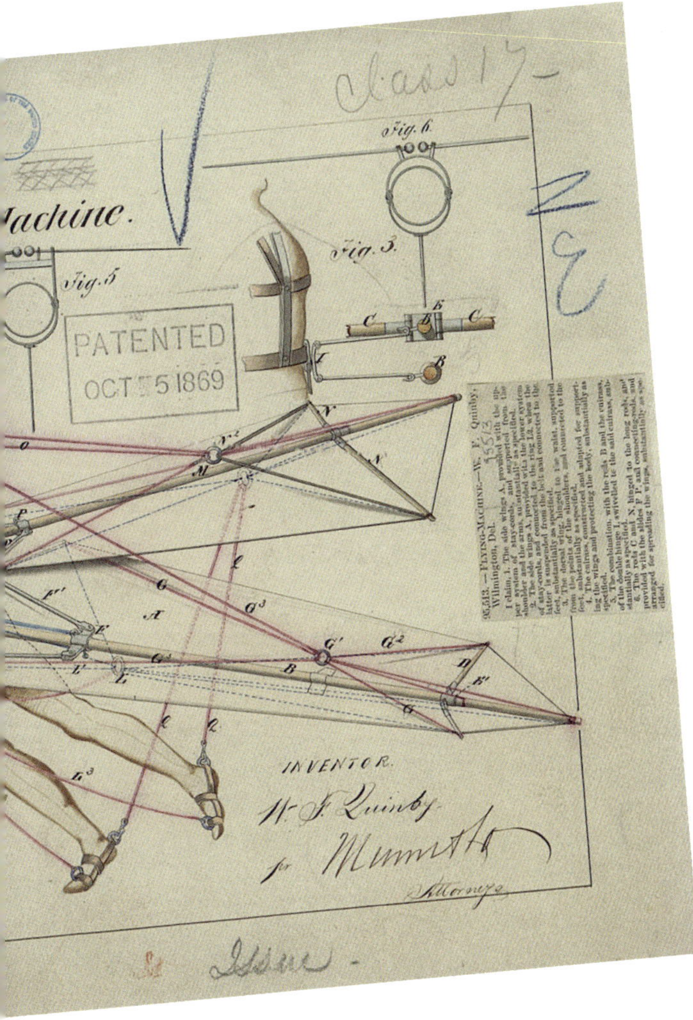

Class 17
Machine.
Fig. 6
Fig. 5
Fig. 3
PATENTED
OCT 5 1869
95,513. — FLYING-MACHINE. — W. F. Quinby, Wilmington, Del.
I claim, 1. The side wings A, provided with the upper system of stay-cords, and supported from the shoulder and the arms, substantially as specified.
2. The side wings A, provided with the lower system of stay-cords, and connected to the ring L2, when the latter is suspended from the belt and connected to the feet, substantially as specified.
3. The dorsal wing, hinged to the waist, supported from the points of the shoulders, and connected to the feet, substantially as specified.
4. The cuirass, constructed and adapted for supporting the wings and protecting the body, substantially as specified.
5. The combination, with the rods B and the cuirass, of the double hinge I, swivelled to the said cuirass, substantially as specified.
6. The rods C and N, hinged to the long rods, and provided with the slides P P, and connecting-rods, and arranged for spreading the wings, substantially as specified.
INVENTOR.
W. F. Quinby
for Munn & Co
Attorneys
Issue

In 1908, German apothecary, inventor, and photographer Julius Neubronner received a patent for his "Method of and Means for Taking Photographs of Landscapes from Above."

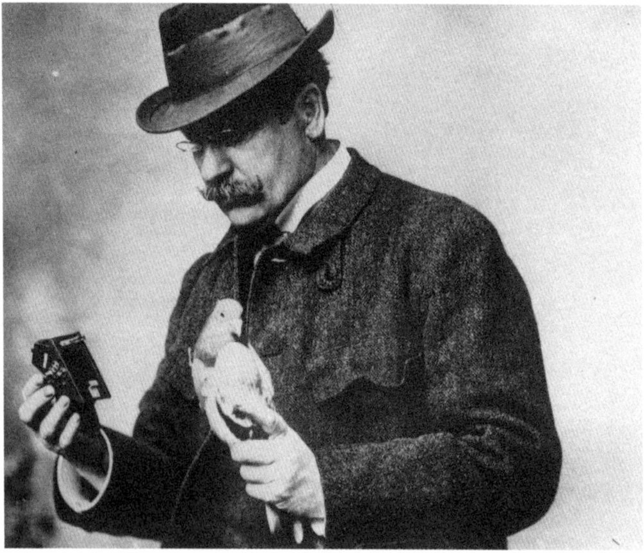

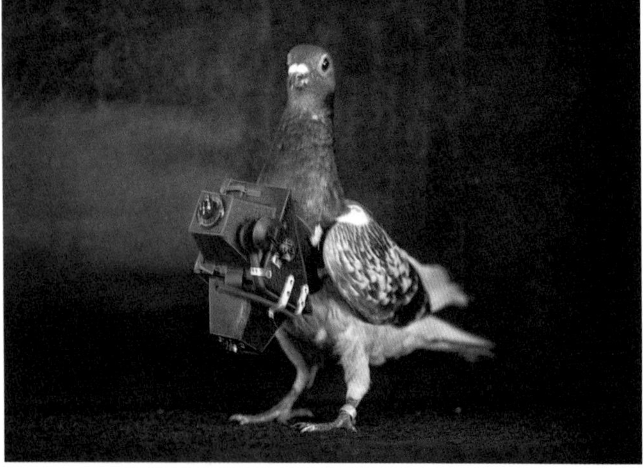

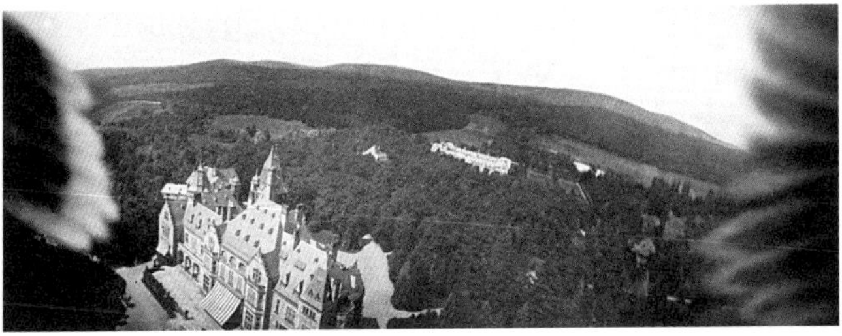

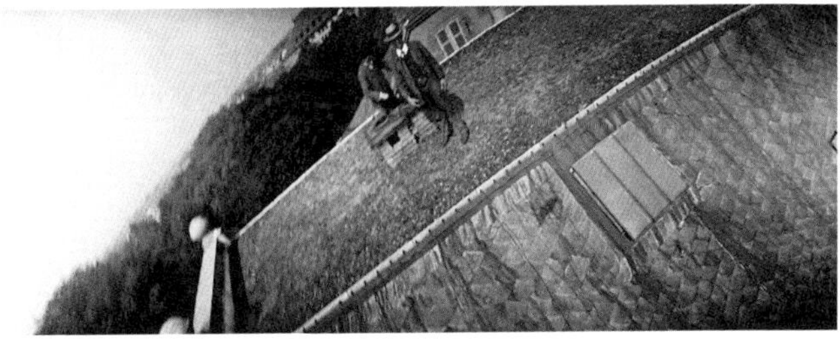

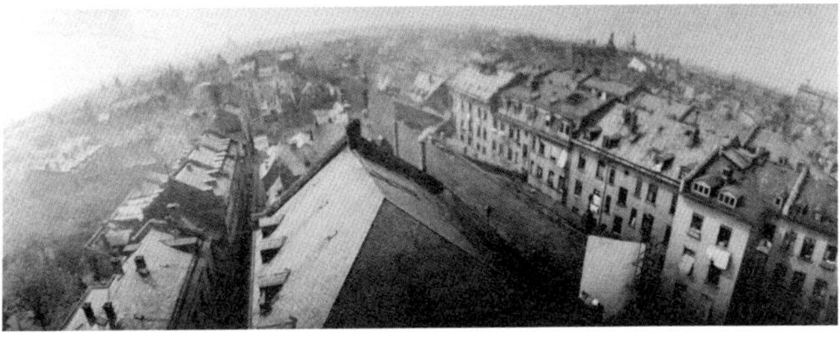

Mohamed Abdel Ghani el-Gamasy, an Egyptian field marshal (with binoculars in hand), during the 1973 Arab–Israeli War.

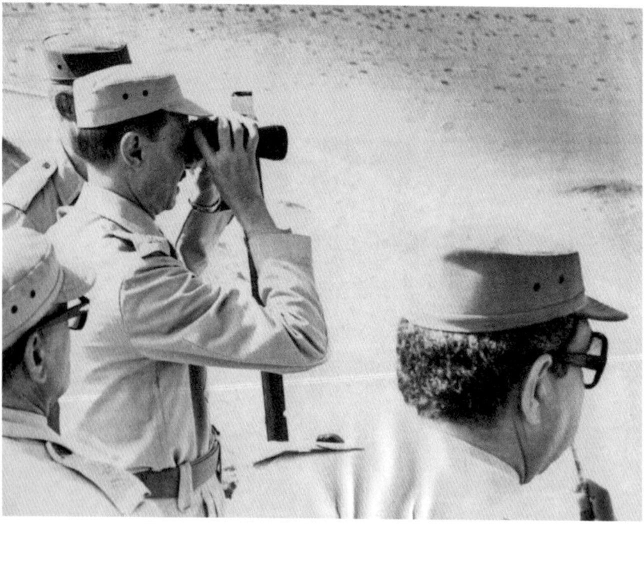

Last preparation before first tactical mission across the Suez Canal in 1969. To the left is Major Shabtai Brill from the Israeli Intelligence Corps, an innovator of the tactical UAV.

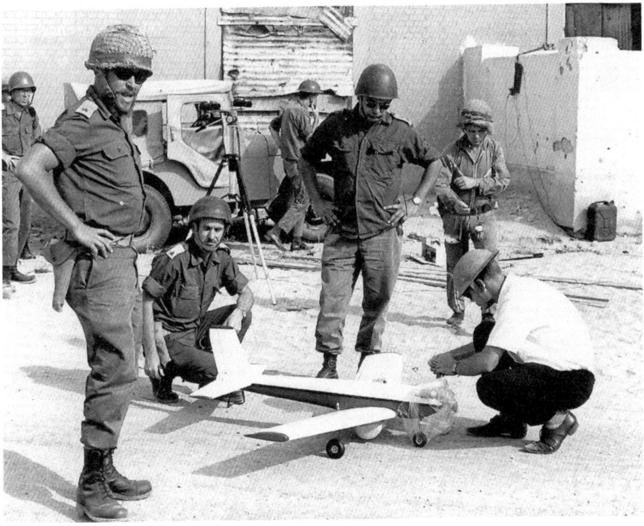

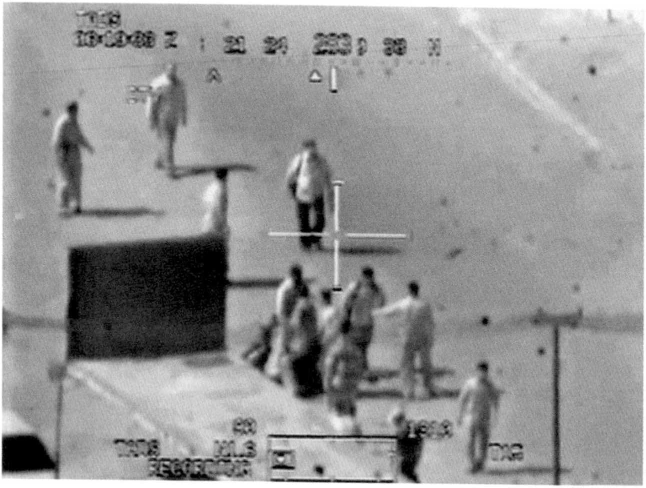

“Eleven people can be seen here. Namir appears to be talking with one of the men while Saeed trails behind.”

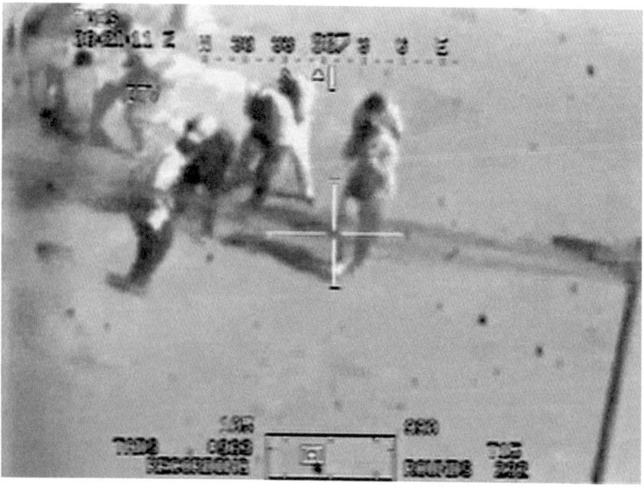

“The men try to cover as the first rounds of shots hit them from the Apache helicopter.”

Opposite, Gunsight footage of the July 12, 2007, airstrike in Baghdad that led to multiple civilian deaths. The footage was subsequently leaked by Chelsea Manning in 2010 to the online whistleblower site WikiLeaks, who titled it *Collateral Murder*.

Below, In 2011, engineers at the laboratory at Festo, a German industrial control and automation company based in Esslingen am Neckar, constructed a bionic "SmartBird" capable of taking off and flying autonomously by flapping its wings like a herring gull.

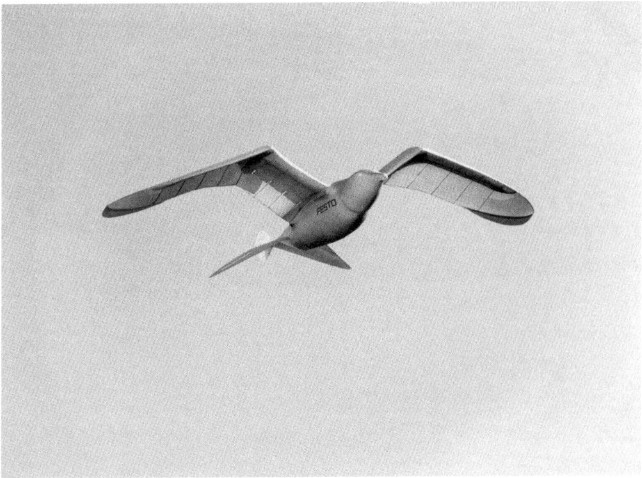

A villager holds a suspected surveillance drone that crashed in Chaman, the capital of Qilla Abdullah District in Balochistan Province, Pakistan, in August 2012.

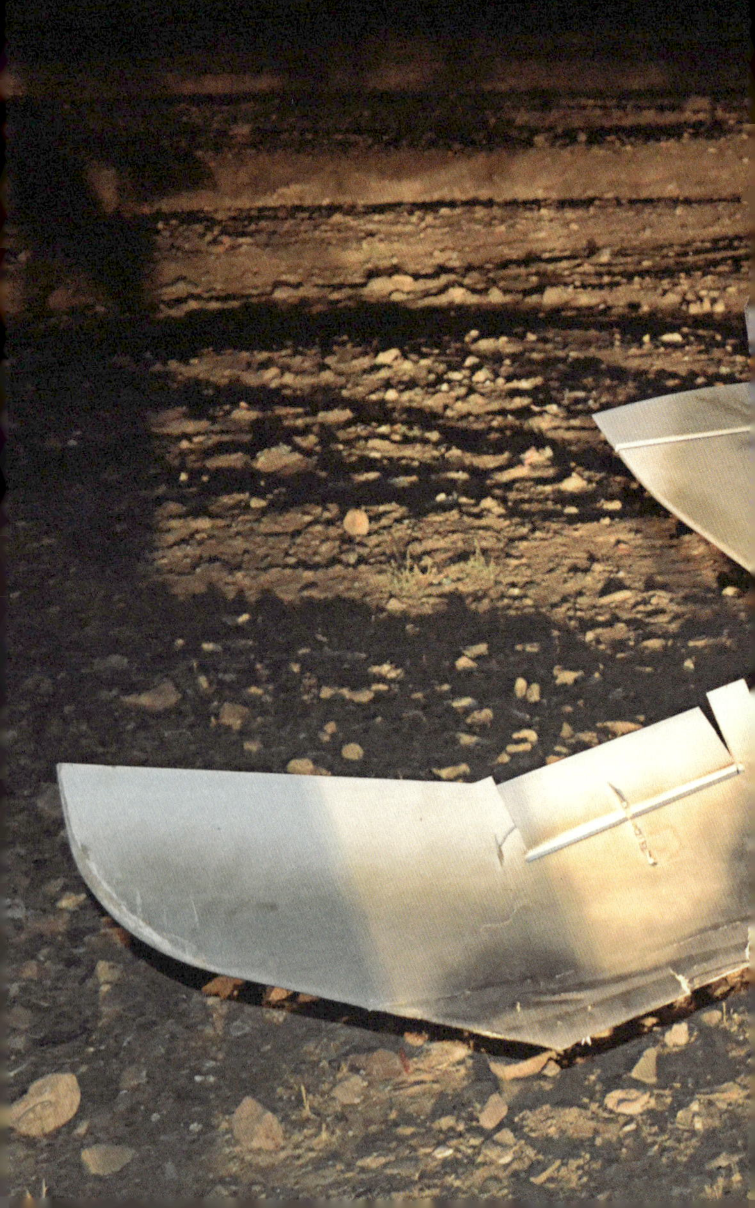

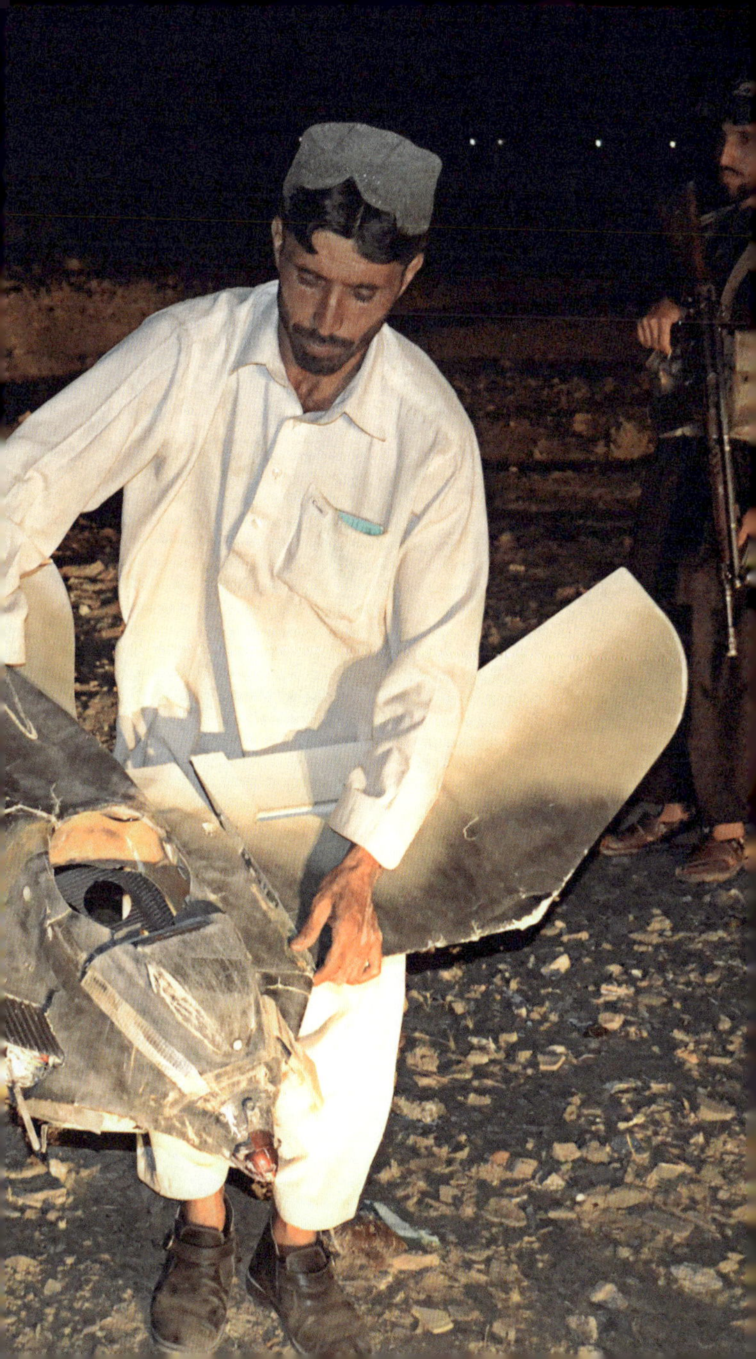

When American army strategists imagine what drones will be like in twenty-five years, they begin by getting an infographist to create a composite image of a typical Arab town, complete with mosque, other buildings, and palm trees.
—Grégoire Chamayou, *Drone Theory*

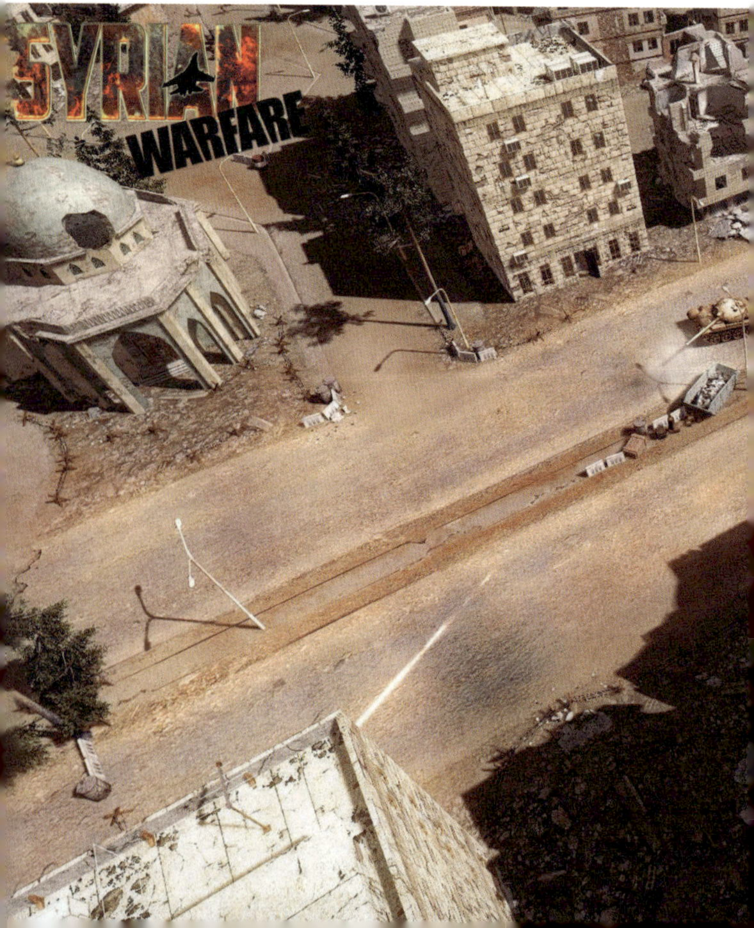

Below, Syrian Warfare is an RTS (Real Time Strategy) video game that was released in February 2017 by a Russian developer named Cats Who Play.

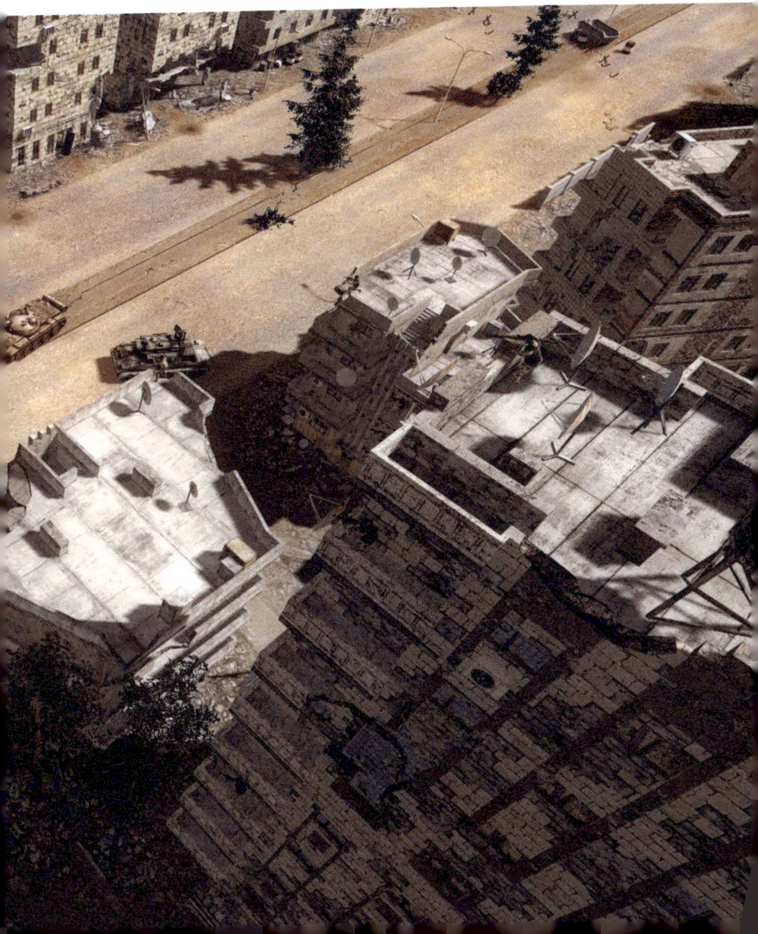

Just Because You're Paranoid Doesn't Mean They Aren't after You

Heba Y. Amin in conversation with Laura Poitras

Heba Y. Amin My work questions states of paranoia in contemporary society. It began with a media story: a migratory stork is detained in Egypt and accused of being a spy. I was not only struck by the absurdity of it, but also by the ways in which the story was decontextualized from any reality that might explain it. Paranoia does not happen in a void; it has to come from somewhere. I never imagined when I started my research that it would lead me to narrate the socio- and geopolitical history of the region. You've been on the FBI watch list: How do you deal with paranoia?

Laura Poitras I can't talk about paranoia without talking about power relationships. Paranoia is this thing you imagine could be possible but can't prove it is happening. From my experience, paranoia is an internalization of state power. There's the great beginning of George Orwell's *1984* where Winston Smith wants to write in his journal but has to crawl to the corner of his room in order to express himself because of the cameras that are ever present. There have definitely been times—from 2011 up until 2016—where I really felt uncertain about the limits of how and where I was being surveilled. Where did the surveillance begin, and where did it end? Sometimes I resist the use of the word "paranoia"; it's not being paranoid to say I'm being watched because I have evidence that I'm being watched. I have my FBI files.[1] Is that then paranoia if you're thinking about state surveillance or government surveillance?

HYA It becomes a very ambiguous term in that sense. Somehow paranoia implies an element of fiction.

LP Yes, I'm sympathetic to the people who didn't trust the stork. Not so much to the people who were imprisoning him, but this question of why should they trust a strange bird? Can we trust that it's just a stork somebody is monitoring for its migration path, or could it have a listening device on it? I think it's a psychological internalization of power that then breeds narratives. And those narratives can get really off the rails, or they can be based in reality. When FBI files of activists are released after people die, you sometimes learn half the people around them were actually informants, and you begin to understand where that paranoia comes from. If you think about Egypt and the intelligence agencies that go after people, that these kinds of stories would emerge is not surprising; it becomes a psychological question to navigate.

HYA I think it brings together a lot of emotional elements: fear, skepticism, cynicism, and variations on those different emotions ...

LP And doubt. People think you're a little crazy. It does create this complex set of paradoxes.

HYA What's interesting is that you deal quite directly with surveillance. I'm curious how you confront that within yourself. In your work, you focus on surveillance, but you are also under surveillance. Have you found your limits? Or how do you navigate that?

LP I make work that I am able to communicate through, so the navigation is expression—artistic expression—and that gives the work some sort of an outlet so that it is not just an internal feedback loop. But it becomes a little bit of a split-personality thing. When I sued the government to get my FBI files, they resisted for a long time, but then finally I got hundreds of pages of my files. I was so excited to have them because: a) they were proof—so I could say, okay,

FBI guys are going to my film screenings; plus: b) it was really great material. My first reaction was that I was excited because it confirmed something I already knew, but then it also gave me great material to work with. I went into work mode: this is awesome. I didn't go: this is terrifying. I'm not sure if that's just a defense mechanism or because I was not surprised.

HYA Did you find anything unusual or striking in your files?

LP The logic of how they built this case was really crazy. I was in Iraq making the film *My Country, My Country*, and after it was released in 2006, they started the investigation. In the FBI documents, I could see that they were basing their analysis on having watched the film and not on anything that had happened while I was in Iraq. There were two things at the basis of their investigation: 1) I was filming on a roof, which is true, and I never denied that; and 2) that I was on the roof to film an attack on the US military, which is 100 percent false. I never filmed an attack. I licensed a clip of archival footage from a news organization and edited it in my film. This juxtaposition later initiated an investigation.

I was very disturbed that they opened a grand jury and subpoenaed multiple companies from my personal records. It's all redacted so I could only assume it was my bank, my credit cards, email accounts—all that personal information. Seeing those documents was new information to process; that was new to me. I knew that I was on a watch list, but I didn't know that people were calling for a grand jury to investigate, or that all my personal records had been turned over to the government.

HYA That must have been a sobering moment.

LP One of the documents describes when I moved offices, so there was physical surveillance. I think many people assume their electronics are surveilled, that's just a given, but what other listening devices and/or cameras are in your living space? That's the line that feels so profoundly invasive.

HYA That must be very strange and scary. But I love this idea that you were excited about the FBI material as content. It makes me think of Sophie Calle's project where she hires a private investigator to follow and spy on her, but the material ends up being too boring, relaying the banality of her everyday life. You, however, have the added narrative of the kind of content you're dealing with, the NSA leaks. It then becomes something profoundly different. Have you ever really felt truly afraid?

LP I was truly afraid. When I started getting emails from Ed [Edward Snowden], I had tinnitus for at least two years. Have you ever had tinnitus? It's a ringing in the ear, and it's almost as if you can hear your body's adrenaline. That's how I would describe it. It's a constant ringing; your nervous system tweaking out. And for me, it was a complete correlation between receiving his emails, imagining the consequences, and knowing the global scale of what the repercussions could be. And also not knowing, because of the list of things to worry about was long. It included every government in the world, every contractor, a lot of things to imagine. When I left Hong Kong in 2013 and returned to Berlin, I learned that a journalist I was working with in Germany was notified by German intelligence that he was being followed. The surveillance was so sophisticated in terms of the number of cars following and hand offs being made that the German intelligence didn't even know which countries were involved. If I had to take a guess,

I think it was probably Israeli intelligence. It raised other questions though, like were intelligence agencies putting rings of protection to keep others away? Things were so heightened for a certain amount of time when the NSA documents were first published and the US didn't have any idea of what had actually been leaked. They still don't seem to have much of a handle on it. So, yeah, that was scary.

HYA I can't imagine.

LP But you can. Because in Egypt you know people are being arrested.

HYA You're right. It is hard to wrap my head around the complexities of how these infrastructures actually work. Of course, we all know they're there, and I think in many ways our lack of understanding of the inner workings of them is what allows us to cope. I don't know how to process it. It's deeply scary and disturbing, and so this is why, for me, the other way to cope with this material is to bring in the element of humor as a way of talking about it.

LP I was thinking about these other questions you were asking about positionality—all my work up until now has been about looking at power, and particularly the impact of US power and how it's being used globally. There are certain things—because I am a US citizen, because I can hire a lawyer, because I am white—that allow me to push the edges in a way that somebody else couldn't without much worse consequences. It is my government that started the war in Iraq, that is doing mass surveillance, that is holding people in Guantánamo, and those are all things that trace back to my country. There are choices I've made that created risk, but those are also all choices. As opposed to, for example, people who I've made work about being in circumstances that are not a choice. The violence is being inflicted and people don't have an option, they don't have an exit.

HYA This question of positionality is so important. I'm often struck by how often people are careless regarding this matter. I think in your work it is quite clear. You critique your own government, but it is often in these other geographies. I'm curious how you engage with those kinds of spaces. Where do you see yourself in those spaces?

LP The films I've made in Iraq and Yemen were very much about trying to create a record of America post-9/11 and how it was being played out. The film made in Iraq was not just a film about an Iraqi family, but it looked under the hood of the occupation. It was always first about the American military. I had not set out to make a film that was just focused on Iraqis—it was also going to be about the US military. Then I felt like that was mirroring their worldview in terms of how we perceive the country. My interest was in US power and documenting its global impact. I've become more present in my work because I get pulled into the narratives over time, but when I was filming in Iraq and Yemen, it felt important for me at that time that I was not in front of the camera and position myself in the work in less obvious ways. How you shoot, the choices you make, the juxtaposition, are all positions to be interpreted and read. It's not like the US doesn't have plenty of blood on its hands historically, but the establishment of Guantánamo in 2002 and the release of the torture memos there, as well as the build up to the Iraq War, felt like enormous shifts in my lifetime, and I felt like I wanted to document them. That's what compelled me to work outside of a US context, rather than an urge to go to another culture and document the abuses of foreign power. I feel there's so much important work for me as an American to do, and that I have an access or privilege that other people don't and that's important to focus on.

There's a document called "Project for a New American Century," which was written at the end of the Cold War in the early 1990s.[2] It described America as a unilateral superpower that no longer needs alliances to take over the map. It was a lot about resources. It seems it became a playbook after 9/11 for a lot of foreign-policy decisions. That's why my work went in that direction.

HYA One of the things I really appreciate about your work is that it activates spaces that have long-reaching arms in terms of impact. I was reading about your 2018 work *Signal Flow* and the investigative report—written by Nick Turse, Henrik Moltke, and Alice Speri—which was published that same year in the *Intercept* about the drones being launched from Sicily to Libya.[3] I wanted to ask you about the ways in which you were addressing the gaze of surveillance and turning it against itself through drone footage. Can you talk a little bit more about this as a strategy?

LP There are limitations. When I was initially invited to exhibit in Manifesta 12, I felt like the theme had nothing to do with my work. It was again this issue of positionality and I didn't feel like I could contribute, so I didn't accept the invitation. Then I started to do some research with Henrik Moltke, a journalist I've been collaborating with on several projects since 2013, and we discovered that the base in Sicily is essentially owned by the US military and is becoming a replacement for other bases that have been particularly politicized, namely, Ramstein, which the US had been using as a relay point for its drone strikes. After discovering this, we decided to take part. Henrik and I have presented our work in art-world or museum contexts, which lets us pair that with journalism. I feel that is important because some of the information we uncovered is newsworthy and should be presented as such. I've been interested in that as a methodology and partly as a strategy because institutions don't always feel comfortable talking about classified information. In other words, we can launch something in the news at the same time as we put it in the museum. It's a strategy I really like. The project at Manifesta had multiple parts. We focused on Sigonella base, which is being used for the signal relay for drone attacks.[4] This was in the original reporting that was published in the *Intercept*. He was the first to report that armed drones were taking off from Sigonella and being flown over Libya. There's also another base in Sicily that's part of a global network of four nodes linking a communication system for the military to use if all other communication systems fail. It's one of these hubs that is in the middle of nowhere, surrounded by a fence. So, we flew a drone over it.

HYA Was that easy to do?

LP I have to credit Henrik and the drone operator we were working with. We scouted the location and found that it wasn't heavily guarded by military. We filmed first on the perimeter and then ultimately over the base, using drones to document it. My friend, a human-rights lawyer, asked this question: How do you feel about using the tools (drones) to document—what are the contradictions there? I think that's an important question or set of critiques. I think for what I was trying to do it was the best, or only, tool to use because one cannot access these bases to show what is there. Our strategy was a sort of "fuck you, we're watching too." I think this kind of countersurveillance flips the tables a little bit.

HYA Was there any response to that? Do you think as a methodology it is a viable strategy?

LP I think I'd call it more of a tactic than a strategy. I make films about occupation. This doesn't put an end to the occupation, but I felt it was important to have a historical record of what happened there. I do think there are interventions that are meaningful, but I think the question of the larger strategy is part of a bigger set of questions. Are artists going to be the ones to have the answers? How do you feel about that?

HYA I'm also interested in using tools against themselves and positioning myself to problematize these tools to begin with. I ask what the potential of changing the narrative is if we openly position ourselves within political and hierarchical structures that are highly problematic. As an artist, I am sometimes troubled by the content I'm dealing with, but feel a need to understand the logic and roles I critique to actively unfold and break apart discourse. By traversing the boundaries between investigative journalism that exists on platforms like the *Intercept* and the artistic work that you exhibit in a museum, do you feel you are able to activate these spaces differently? How do those dialogues differ?

LP I would also add to that a third space, which is somewhat different than the art world or journalism: long-form documentary. I think they activate differently. With the NSA documents and Edward Snowden story, I worked in journalism, documentary, and gallery/museum spaces. I wasn't doing print journalism before Snowden contacted me. He came forward and I had an obligation to make sure the information, which was clearly newsworthy, found an outlet in the major newspapers. Collaborating with news organizations was foreign to me, and it also felt very constricting. Making *Citizenfour* (2014) was an obvious and necessary extension of my work. For my 2016 exhibition at the Whitney Museum, "Astro Noise," I worked with the NSA material in a visual, experiential, and contemplative way. I really do love doing installation work. I worry that it exists in a rarified space and that space, almost by definition, can be co-opted. There's a danger. How does one do something that is confrontational and political but also exists in an institution? Are there institutions you would not present your work at?

HYA I certainly always consider the politics of the institution I am working with, and negotiate the ways in which I think I can subvert that space. Either way, being an artist and working in the art world makes us complicit in a lot of things that we don't want to be complicit in. The next step, in my opinion, is to make sure we can confront it in our work. That seems to be the right strategy, for me anyway. I also think it is important to make things transparent.

LP I very much agree with you, I don't think we should work for political ends. There are other means to create political change but I don't think art should bear that responsibility. I do believe, however, that visual representations do have a capacity or ability to reach people in ways that other forms of information don't. I believe in that.

HYA Yes. Regarding the impact of images, there's a question I want to ask you through a quote by Paul Virilio where he addresses "the deadly harmony that always establishes itself between the functions of eye and weapon."[5] I'm really struck by this quote. It leaves a lingering visual in my head. Going back to the visuals of drones and the bird's-eye view, which is meant to somehow be more precise but also dehumanizing, what do you think about these kinds of images? Can they ever be emancipatory? Can they be disconnected from their original construct of violence? Do you think they ever have a potential to be humanizing?

LP I do think there are ways one could potentially engage, but I would argue it's maybe more about what you do on the ground, and what you make visible. As you were reading that quote, my mind associated it in a different direction—you have this obsession with the aerial view, which I totally get, and I have this obsession with primary document evidence: I want to see it. The US government had ninety-two torture tapes in their possession, which were destroyed. Were they really destroyed? How can we see them? There's a whole library of files at Guantánamo that details what happened to detainees: What happens if that goes public? People who commit violence often document their violence acts, and that's usually the only documentary evidence we'll ever have. A perpetrator of violence is often his or her own documentarian. How can we liberate or find those images, and what do those images say about the act of violence and power and the eye? If we could see those images, would they change? I have this hope that it would, that if we could see what's being done in our name that it would change. There is plenty of evidence to show that, perhaps, this is not the case. We see lots of things, lots of violence, and still it continues.

HYA How do you think that has transpired since Snowden's NSA leaks, since those became visible? That's five years ago now. Do you think the visibility and the seeing of those files have changed anything?

LP Yes and no. It shifted consciousness about how we use our devices. Most people now understand that their communication is subject to being monitored and what that means on a truly internalized way. This global shift of consciousness is pretty profound. Did it change policies and governments? No. You see less evidence of that. I often ask what could have been done differently with the Snowden releases, and I have my own criticisms of the choices I made.

HYA Given all that we now know about the surveillance system and recent events that have unfolded with Julian Assange being arrested and Chelsea Manning being in jail, do you think that we can play any role in subverting that gaze of surveillance?

LP We're sitting here, after that moment, and now they're both in prison.[6] It's really sad on many levels. I'm profoundly grateful to the work that Julian and WikiLeaks have done, and what they opened up as a different, more adversarial form of journalism. This doesn't put aside the critiques I've made in other places. WikiLeaks's impact is extraordinary, and I wish we were at a different juncture. A very small group of people put enormous pressure on governments all over the world through information. And I think that has had a transformative impact, so I guess I do believe that there are ways to challenge power. I think about the beginning of television when images from the Vietnam War were being shown; those images were one of the reasons the war ended, because they were so brutal and bloody. How does war look now when we see it on television? Very different than that. Something is opened, our perception shifts, and then technologies become co-opted.

HYA I suppose that's a more hopeful way to look at it, by emphasizing these shifts.

LP The leverage of new technologies, even though we see them as tools of surveillance and state power, also allow people to organize, communicate anonymously, and resist.

1 Poitras has surmised that she was subjected to monitoring and surveillance by the US government following a wire transfer she sent in 2006 to an Iraqi medical doctor and Sunni political candidate, Riyadh al-Adhadh, who was the subject of her documentary *My Country, My Country*. For fuller details of her attempts to reveal why the US government had placed her under surveillance and its impact on her work and life, see Laura Poitras, *Astro Noise: A Survival Guide for Living under Total Surveillance* (New York: Yale University Press, 2016).

2 The Project for a New American Century (PNAC) is a neoconservative think tank formed in the spring of 1997 and founded by William Kristol, an American neoconservative political analyst, and Robert Kagan, an American historian and foreign-policy commentator. For details of the formation and activities of PNAC, see http://www.historycommons.org/entity.jsp?entity=project_for_the_new_american_century. PNAC ceased to function in 2006 and was replaced by the Foreign Policy Initiative, also cofounded by Kristol and Kagan in 2009. The Foreign Policy Initiative was dissolved in 2017.

3 See Nick Turse, Henrik Moltke, and Alice Speri, "Secret War," *Intercept*, June 21, 2018, https://theintercept.com/2018/06/20/libya-us-drone-strikes/. *Signal Flow* is a work by Laura Poitras for Manifesta 12, which took place in Palermo in 2018. See http://m12.manifesta.org/signal-flow-2018/.

4 The Air Force's 324th Expeditionary Reconnaissance Squadron and its MQ-1 Predator drones began operating from Naval Air Station Sigonella in Italy on March 25, 2011. For full details of the Sigonella Naval Air Station in Sicily, see Turse, Moltke, and Speri, "Secret War."

5 Paul Virilio, *War and Cinema: The Logistics of Perception* (London: Verso, 1984), 69.

6 Reportedly in ill-health, as of January 2020, Assange is incarcerated in HM Prison Belmarsh, a prison in Thamesmead, South East London. In March 2020, a judge ordered the release of Chelsea Manning from the federal detention center in Alexandria, Virginia, where she has been held since last May for refusing to testify against Julian Assange before a grand jury. In December 2019, the *Guardian* reported that Nils Melzer, the UN special rapporteur on torture, had written a letter in November 2019 accusing the US government of using torture against Manning. Melzer wrote that Manning was being subjected to "an open-ended, progressively severe measure of coercion fulfilling all the constitutive elements of torture or other cruel, inhuman or degrading treatment or punishment." Melzer, quoted in Edward Helmore, "Top UN Official Accuses US of Torturing Chelsea Manning," *Guardian*, December 31, 2019, https://www.theguardian.com/us-news/2019/dec/31/chelsea-manning-us-torture-un-official-wikileaks.

Pages 106–11: Documentation of General Allenby while he led the British Empire's Egyptian Expeditionary Force (EEF), during the campaign to capture Jerusalem from the Ottoman Empire.

With General Allenby's Advance on Jerusalem

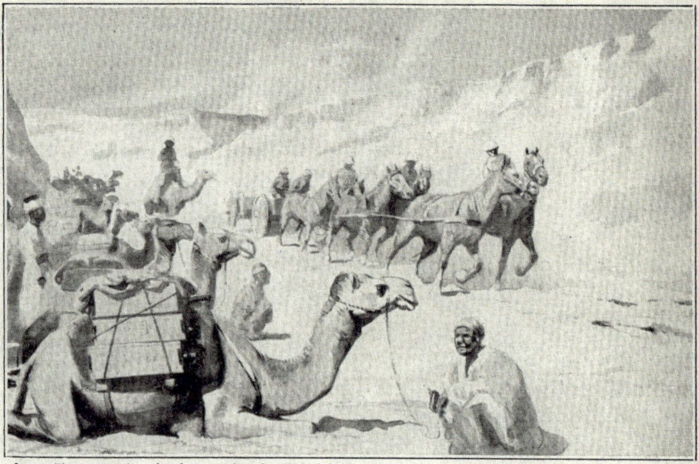

Ammunition waggons, hurrying along a sandy wady with shells for the guns, passing a convoy of ammunition-laden camels "barracked" for rest. The dried-up river-courses of Palestine provided useful cover for the movement of guns and supplies to the first line.

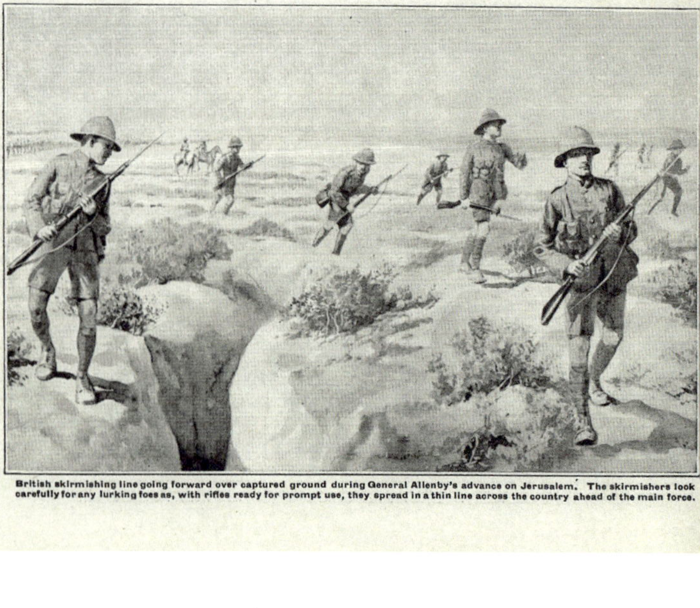

British skirmishing line going forward over captured ground during General Allenby's advance on Jerusalem. The skirmishers look carefully for any lurking foes as, with rifles ready for prompt use, they spread in a thin line across the country ahead of the main force.

Light Relief Amid the Grim Tasks of War

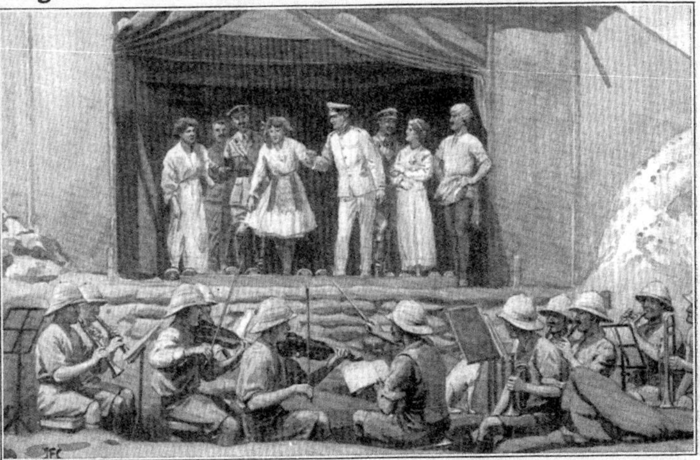

The spirit of play informing men who were engaged in the stern tasks of war on the Palestine front, where a play, "The Rose of Gaza," was successfully produced, the stage being erected alongside a trench in which members of the orchestra were seated. The play was entirely got up and performed by members of the Essex Regiment.

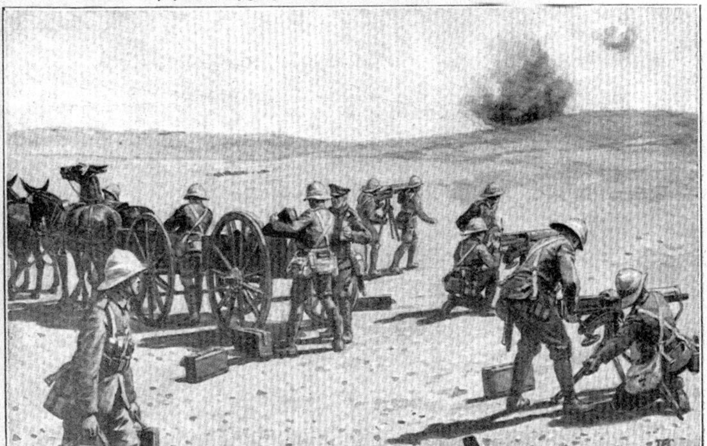

With the machine-guns during Sir Edmund Allenby's triumphant advance. Men of a machine-gun section engaged in unloading and getting their weapons into immediate action as soon as they found themselves within range of the retreating Turks. Before the end of February, 1918, General Allenby had captured Jericho and forced the enemy into a further retreat to the north.

3063

General Allenby's Great Advance in Palestine

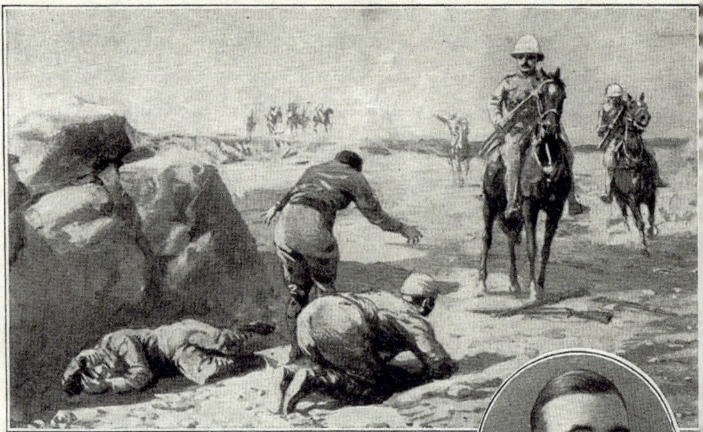

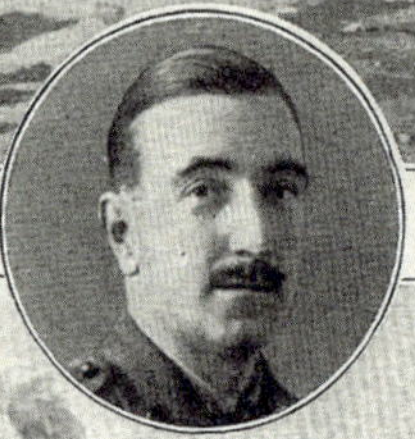

Rounding up Turkish refugees during the Palestine advance. Inset: Lieut.-Colonel H. A. Gray Cheape, leader of the brilliant charge of the Worcestershire and Warwickshire Yeomanry in Palestine early in November, 1917, when they charged a dozen of the enemy guns, sabred the gunners, and captured the batteries. [*Photo: Yevonde.*

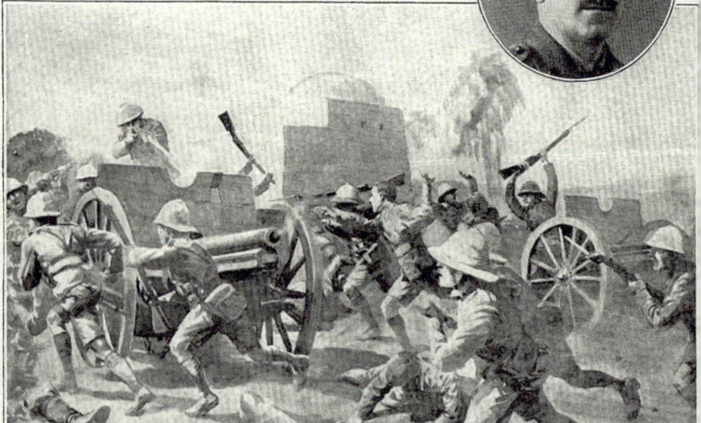

Infantry charge on the guns at Tel-el-Sheria in the Palestine advance. At a point where four enemy field-guns remained in action a battalion commander called for volunteers and, leading them, dashed over the broken ground, killed the gunners, and captured the guns.

St. George and Jerusalem

End of Four Centuries of Turkish Misrule in the Holy City

NO event in the Great War made a more instant appeal to humanity than the surrender of Jerusalem to the British forces under General Allenby, who formally entered the Holy City on December 11th, 1917.

It was a small matter, comparatively speaking, that this victory marked the failure of Falkenhayn to retain the city for the Turks, who had held dominion over it since 1517. Far more significant was the fact that the city was surrounded, not assaulted, with the result that, for Jew, Moslem, and Christian alike, the Holy Places have been saved from destruction. There had been talk in German papers of "the new Cross on Calvary—a 16in. gun," but happily it came to nothing.

General Allenby succeeded where Napoleon failed. In 1799 the Emperor, after occupying Egypt, crossed the desert, stormed Gaza and Jaffa, and laid siege to Acre. Failing here, however, he retreated westwards, and the Crescent remained supreme over the Holy City. Richard Cœur de Lion had been no more successful in 1192 than was Napoleon in 1799.

Jerusalem—or rather the custody of the Holy Places in it—was the cause of the Crimean War, the Greek and Latin ecclesiastics failing to agree as to their respective rights. At that period Russia was endeavouring by peaceful penetration to secure that hold on Jerusalem which the Orthodox Greeks had long insisted was their due. This peaceful penetration was fostered by monetary grants to the Greek monasteries and to Russian pilgrimages.

3,500 Years of History

The Orthodox Greeks were taught that the Archangel Michael, mentioned in the Scriptures as the predestined deliverer of the Promised Land, would be represented by a Russian prince, and that this prince would, in due time, enter the Holy City in triumph through the closed-up Golden Gate.

It is a remarkable circumstance that Jew, Christian, and Moslem look for the Last Judgment to take place in the Valley of Jehoshaphat, lying beneath the Eastern Wall of Jerusalem.

The capture of Hebron a few days before the fall of Jerusalem recalls the Biblical story of Abraham's purchase there of the sepulchre of his wife. Thus the first possession of the Jewish people in the Holy Land was a grave. A grave is, perhaps, too sombre a description to apply to the last resting-place of the beautiful Sarah, for the place was a natural cave, set in a pleasant field, and sheltered by whispering trees.

Jerusalem is a golden city in one respect only: the glory of its sunshine. The city, which has been rebuilt several times in its 3,500 years of existence, looks down on the plain from a height of between 2,000 and 3,000 feet above the level of the sea. The gently-sloping hills which encircle the Holy City inspired the words of the Psalmist: "As the hills stand about Jerusalem, even so standeth the Lord about His people."

Jerusalem itself is poor, and even mean and small. Within its walls its circumference is but two and a half miles. Its streets are winding lanes. Its sanitation is deplorable. But it contains, in the "Mosque of Omar" (or Dome of the Rock) and the Church of the Holy Sepulchre, buildings striking in themselves and priceless in significance to Moslem and Christian respectively.

Once a city surrounded by verdant and fruitful land, fertility long since passed Jerusalem by. Cultivation was never permitted within its walls. To-day the comparative barrenness of the adjacent hills and valleys finds little compensation in the windowless, one-storied dwellings that have sprung up outside the historic and tower-decked walls.

Apart from its sacred associations to the Christian as the city in which "the footsteps of Revealed Divinity pressed the ground," and where the Sacrament was first instituted, to the Jew as the "City of David," and to the Moslem as the spot whence Mohammed ascended to heaven, Jerusalem saw Solomon in all his glory. Alexander the Great and Pompey the Great left lasting impress here. Cleopatra sought to win the city from Cæsar and Mark Antony. To rescue it from the hands of the Infidel was the purpose of the Crusades, the story of which is enshrined in Tasso's great epic, "La Gerusalemme Liberata," and the romances of Sir Walter Scott. But little of the former glory of the city remains visible to the eye of the modern visitor. It is like a place mourning over departed greatness, watching and waiting for things to be.

JERUSALEM IN HISTORY

	APPROXIMATE DATES
Urusalim an Egyptian fortress	B.C. 1400
Taken by David from the Jebusites	1048
Solomon's Temple built	993
Taken by Shishak, King of Egypt	973
Taken by Jehoash, King of Israel	839
Besieged by Sennacherib	700
Pillaged by Nebuchadnezzar	587
Jews return under Cyrus	536
Second Temple finished	516
Walls rebuilt by Nehemiah	444
Surrendered to Alexander	332
Sacked by Ptolemy I.	323
Sacked by Antigonus of Syria	314
Reverted to Ptolemy	301
Taken by Antiochus III.	203
Sacked by Antiochus IV.	168
Retaken by the Maccabees	165
Taken by Antiochus VII.	133
Taken by Pompey	65
Surrendered to and rebuilt by Herod	37–19
Destroyed by Titus	A.D. 70
Rebuilt by Adrian and named Aelia Capitolina	130–6
Rebellion under Barcocheba	132
Taken by Chosroes II.	614
Recovered by Greek Emperor Heraclius	629
Taken by the Khalif Omar	637
Dome of the Rock erected	691
Conquered by Seljuk Turks	1077
Godfrey of Bouillon's standard on Calvary	1099
Taken by Saladin	1187
Retaken by Turks	1217
Surrendered to Frederick II.	1229
Stormed by Turkish Emir of Kerak	1239
Ransomed by Richard, Earl of Cornwall	1241
Taken by Kharismian Turks for their Egyptian allies	1244
Captured by Turks under Selim I.	1517

Seriousness, solemnity, severity mark its everyday life and aspect. There are no amusements such as cities of the Western world find essential. There are no newspapers. The only bookstalls are without the walls, for the sale of Bibles. Even the children seem affected as by an atmosphere of otherworldliness. There are banks and hotels for the convenience of the pilgrim and the traveller, and a light railway runs from Jaffa to a spot just outside the city, but these are almost the only concessions to western habits and customs.

The Turkish hold on the Holy City has lasted for four centuries, but the soil has no fixed proprietors. Whoever holds Jerusalem must hold it in trust. It is unthinkable that any Power, except Germany, would seek to govern it otherwise than as a trust.

Perhaps it was in the German Emperor's mind to change all this when, to the mild consternation of the Vatican and no little expense to the Sultan, he paid his spectacular visit to Jerusalem in 1898. Arrayed as a Crusader and mounted on a white charger, he rode through an opening specially made in the wall, escorted by troops and Turkish police. The display had its fantastic side, but it marked a stage in the development of the Kaiser's "Drang nach Osten" dream, from which he was destined to experience an unexpected and a rude awakening.

General Allenby's Historic Entry

In striking contrast to the theatrical pageant of 1898 was the entry of General Allenby and the representatives of France, Italy, and the United States nineteen years later. This procession lacked nothing in dignity, but it passed on foot through the Jaffa Gate, where stood guards representing England, Scotland, Ireland, Wales, Australia, New Zealand, India, France, and Italy. The populace received it with every token of goodwill. Guards were posted at the Holy Places in harmony with the Greek and Latin representatives. The "Mosque of Omar" was placed under Moslem control, with cordons of Indian Mohammedans.

General Allenby's proclamation, expressing his desire that every person should pursue his lawful business without fear of interruption, contained these memorable words:

> Since your city is regarded with affection by the adherents of three of the great religions of mankind, and its soil has been consecrated by the prayers and pilgrimages of multitudes of devout people of three religions for many centuries, therefore do I make known to you that every sacred building, monument, holy spot, shrine, traditional site, endowment, pious bequest, or customary place of prayer of whatsoever form of the three religions will be maintained and protected according to the existing customs and beliefs of those to whose faiths they are sacred.

When, at Reading, in 1185, the Patriarch of Jerusalem gave to Henry II. the keys of the city, and said to him, "In thee alone, after God, do the people of the land put their trust," Henry answered, "May our Lord Jesus Christ, the King of Power, be the defender of His people, and we will be His fellow-workers to the utmost of our power." As Archdeacon Hutton reminds us, never till this day has a British Sovereign been able to redeem that promise. In December, 1917, the flag of King George V. floated over the Holy City. The name of George is among the best-beloved in Eastern Christendom, and new interest was aroused in the discovery at Gaza, in October, 1917, of the supposed relics of St. George of Cappadocia, the patron saint of England.

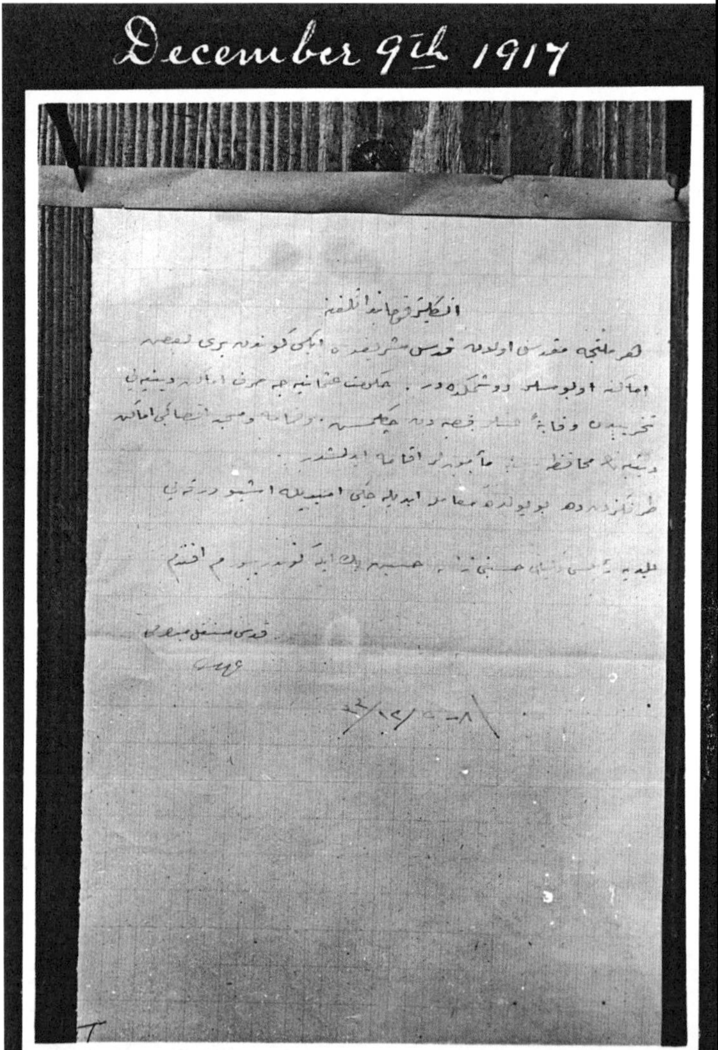
December 9th 1917
Copy of letter of Surrender.

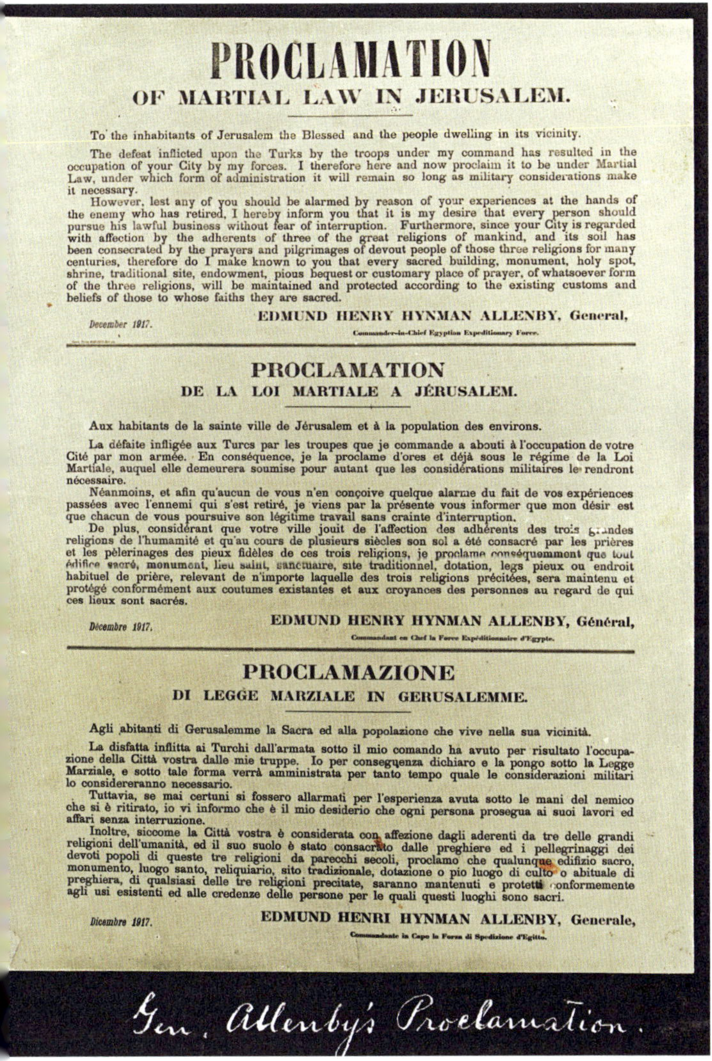

PROCLAMATION

OF MARTIAL LAW IN JERUSALEM.

To the inhabitants of Jerusalem the Blessed and the people dwelling in its vicinity.

The defeat inflicted upon the Turks by the troops under my command has resulted in the occupation of your City by my forces. I therefore here and now proclaim it to be under Martial Law, under which form of administration it will remain so long as military considerations make it necessary.

However, lest any of you should be alarmed by reason of your experiences at the hands of the enemy who has retired, I hereby inform you that it is my desire that every person should pursue his lawful business without fear of interruption. Furthermore, since your City is regarded with affection by the adherents of three of the great religions of mankind, and its soil has been consecrated by the prayers and pilgrimages of devout people of those three religions for many centuries, therefore do I make known to you that every sacred building, monument, holy spot, shrine, traditional site, endowment, pious bequest or customary place of prayer, of whatsoever form of the three religions, will be maintained and protected according to the existing customs and beliefs of those to whose faiths they are sacred.

December 1917. EDMUND HENRY HYNMAN ALLENBY, General,

Commander-in-Chief Egyptian Expeditionary Force.

PROCLAMATION

DE LA LOI MARTIALE A JÉRUSALEM.

Aux habitants de la sainte ville de Jérusalem et à la population des environs.

La défaite infligée aux Turcs par les troupes que je commande a abouti à l'occupation de votre Cité par mon armée. En conséquence, je la proclame d'ores et déjà sous le régime de la Loi Martiale, auquel elle demeurera soumise pour autant que les considérations militaires le rendront nécessaire.

Néanmoins, et afin qu'aucun de vous n'en conçoive quelque alarme du fait de vos expériences passées avec l'ennemi qui s'est retiré, je viens par la présente vous informer que mon désir est que chacun de vous poursuive son légitime travail sans crainte d'interruption.

De plus, considérant que votre ville jouit de l'affection des adhérents des trois grandes religions de l'humamité et qu'au cours de plusieurs siècles son sol a été consacré par les prières et les pèlerinages des pieux fidèles de ces trois religions, je proclame conséquemment que tout édifice sacré, monument, lieu saint, sanctuaire, site traditionnel, dotation, legs pieux ou endroit habituel de prière, relevant de n'importe laquelle des trois religions précitées, sera maintenu et protégé conformément aux coutumes existantes et aux croyances des personnes au regard de qui ces lieux sont sacrés.

Décembre 1917. EDMUND HENRY HYNMAN ALLENBY, Général,

Commandant en Chef la Force Expéditionnaire d'Egypte.

PROCLAMAZIONE

DI LEGGE MARZIALE IN GERUSALEMME.

Agli abitanti di Gerusalemme la Sacra ed alla popolazione che vive nella sua vicinità.

La disfatta inflitta ai Turchi dall'armata sotto il mio comando ha avuto per risultato l'occupazione della Città vostra dalle mie truppe. Io per conseguenza dichiaro e la pongo sotto la Legge Marziale, e sotto tale forma verrà amministrata per tanto tempo quale le considerazioni militari lo considereranno necessario.

Tuttavia, se mai certuni si fossero allarmati per l'esperienza avuta sotto le mani del nemico che si è ritirato, io vi informo che è il mio desiderio che ogni persona prosegua ai suoi lavori ed affari senza interruzione.

Inoltre, siccome la Città vostra è considerata con affezione dagli aderenti da tre delle grandi religioni dell'umanità, ed il suo suolo è stato consacrato dalle preghiere ed i pellegrinaggi dei devoti popoli di queste tre religioni da parecchi secoli, proclamo che qualunque edifizio sacro, monumento, luogo santo, reliquiario, sito tradizionale, dotazione o pio luogo di culto o abituale di preghiera, di qualsiasi delle tre religioni precitate, saranno mantenuti e protetti conformemente agli usi esistenti ed alle credenze delle persone per le quali questi luoghi sono sacri.

Dicembre 1917. EDMUND HENRI HYNMAN ALLENBY, Generale,

Commandante in Capo la Forza di Spedizione d'Egitto.

Gen. Allenby's Proclamation.

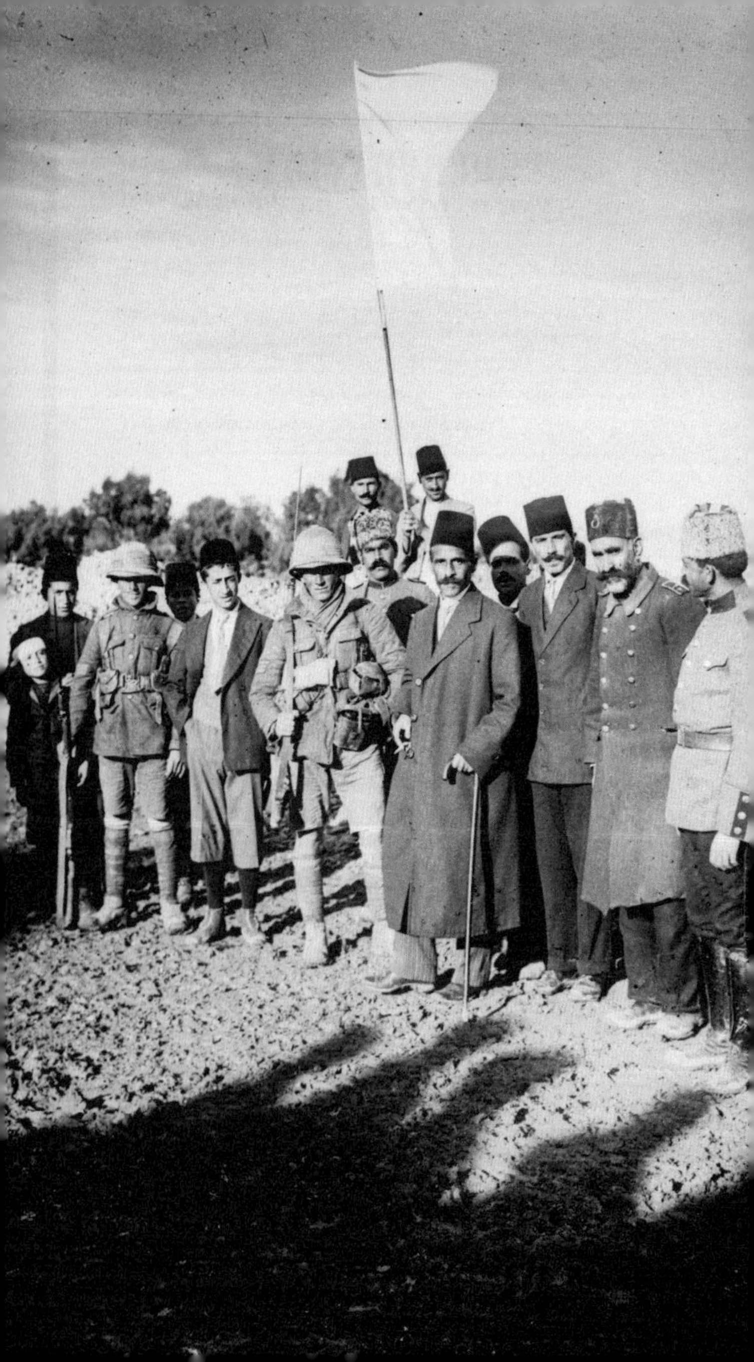

The surrender of Jerusalem to the British Army on December 9, 1917. The mayor of Jerusalem, Hussein Bey al-Husayni (holding a cane), stands next to two British "tommies" (sergeants).

Overleaf, Spread from Vivian Gilbert, *The Romance of the Last Crusade: With Allenby to Jerusalem* (1923).

"Where is General Allah Nebi?" now enquired the man in the red fez.

"'Anged if I know, mister," answered the private.

"I want to surrender the city please. 'Ere are ze keys; it is yours!" went on the stranger, producing a large bunch of keys and waving them before the bewildered Britisher, who now began to think he had fallen amongst lunatics.

"I don't want yer city. I want some heggs for my hofficers!" yelled the disgusted cook.

* * * * * * *

Whilst all these things were happening the major was awaiting anxiously the return of the cook with his breakfast. The other officers also were beginning to feel hungry; as for the colonel, he made a few caustic remarks with reference to brilliant ideas in general and sent for his own servant to take the cook's place.

I happened to be at battalion headquarters when Private Murch, hot and out of breath, arrived.

"Where have you been for the last four hours?" demanded the colonel in a freezing tone.

The perspiring private proceeded to relate his amazing adventures in a rich cockney dialect.

In spite of his rambling and at times incoerent recitation, it dawned on us at last that ne of the greatest events in the history of the orld, for which thousands had given their lives nd for which millions of pounds of English noney had been poured out, had just taken place.

When the man came to the end of his story, he colonel turned to us and said quietly, "Gen-emen, Jerusalem has fallen!"

Then he seized a field telephone, rang up the rigadier, and acquainted him with the startling ews.

Brigadier-General Watson was wildly excited —he was the nearest general to the Holy City nd to him would fall the honour of accepting he surrender: his name would be flashed to very corner of the globe.

"Where's my horse?" he shouted. "Saddle im up immediately and tell the groom to follow ne," and he hurried to his tent for his best red ap and fly whisk.

In a few minutes he was galloping madly up he Jaffa-Jerusalem road followed by an orderly n a mule.

He met the mayor in his carriage outside the affa Gate. The road was now black with peo-le, for everyone in the city was at last aware he Turks had left for good.

Below, Entry of Field Marshal Allenby into Jerusalem, December 11, 1917.

Opposite top, Field Marshal Allenby accepts surrender of Jerusalem officials, January 1, 1917.

Opposite bottom, Allenby enters Jerusalem, magic-lantern glass slide, 1940.

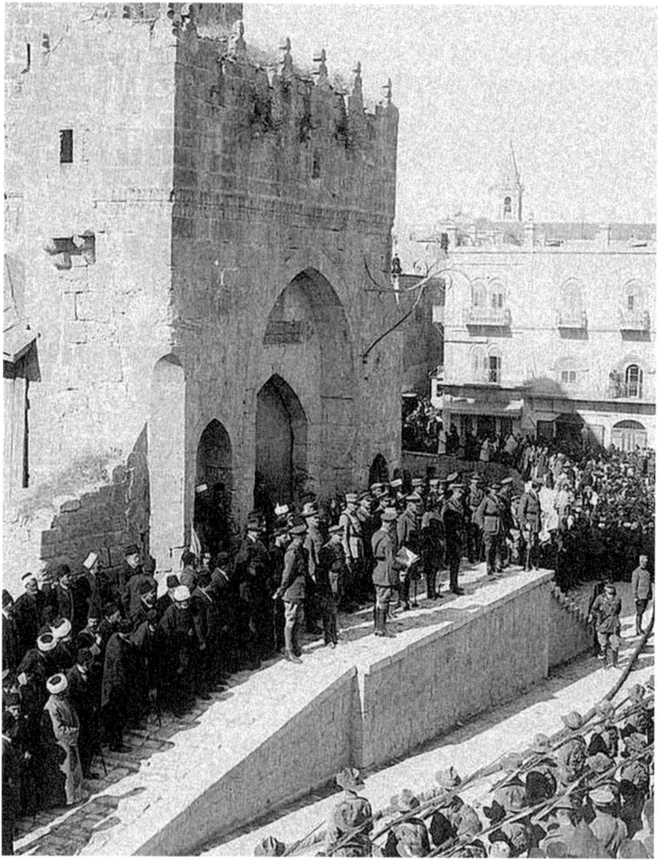

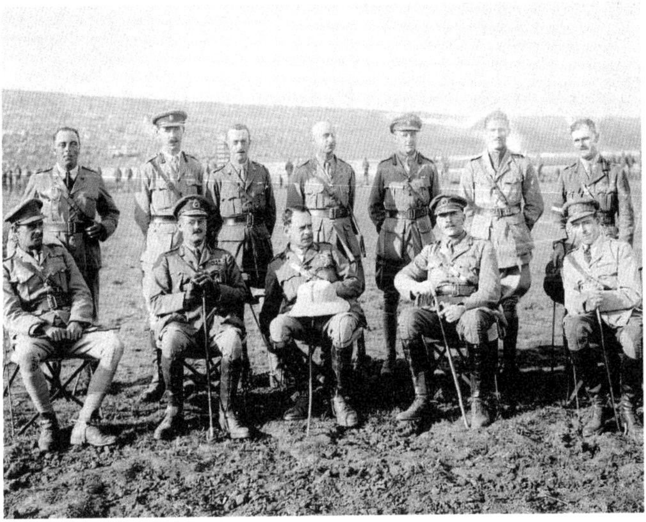

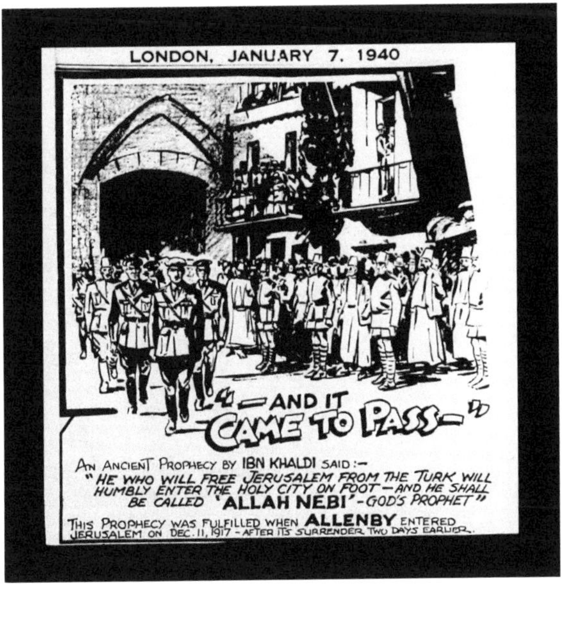
LONDON, JANUARY 7, 1940
"—AND IT CAME TO PASS—"
AN ANCIENT PROPHECY BY IBN KHALDI SAID:—
"HE WHO WILL FREE JERUSALEM FROM THE TURK WILL HUMBLY ENTER THE HOLY CITY ON FOOT—AND HE SHALL BE CALLED 'ALLAH NEBI'-GOD'S PROPHET"
THIS PROPHECY WAS FULFILLED WHEN ALLENBY ENTERED JERUSALEM ON DEC. 11, 1917 - AFTER ITS SURRENDER TWO DAYS EARLIER.

3397

Where British Armies Pressed Forward in the East

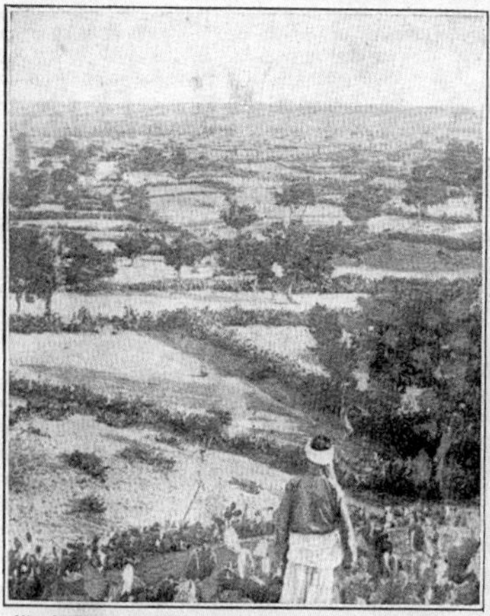

View from one of the hills overlooking Gaza, the capture of which by General Allenby on Nov. 7th, 1917, marked an important stage in the Palestine advance. The hedges are "prickly-pear" cactus.

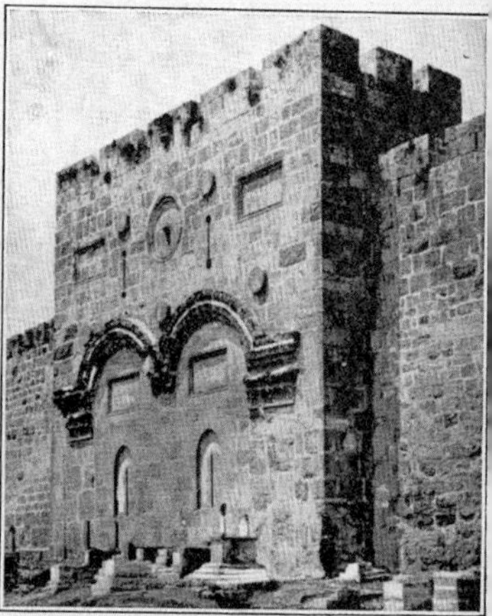

Outside of the Golden Gate in the city wall of Jerusalem. This gate has been kept walled up ever since the time of Herod, close upon two thousand years ago.

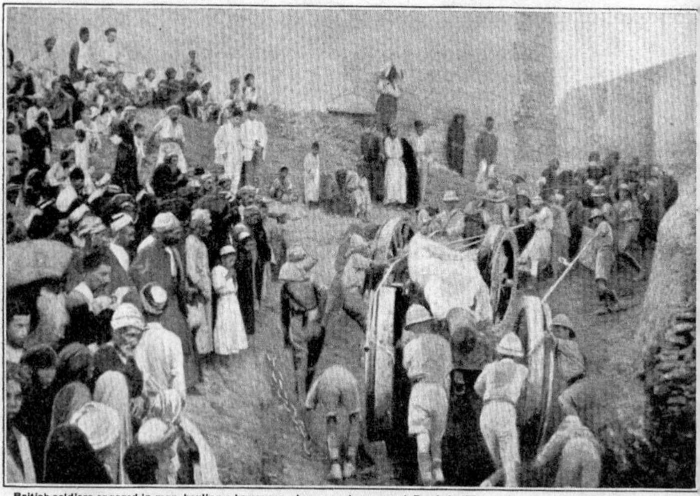

British soldiers engaged in man-hauling a heavy gun along a sunken way at Bagdad. The motley crowd of Arabs, old and young, watch with interest the work of the men who have delivered them from the dominion of the Turk. (British official photograph.)

GENERAL ALLENBY IN JERUSALEM: THE PROCLAMATION: NOTABLES.

OFFICIAL PHOTOGRAPHS.

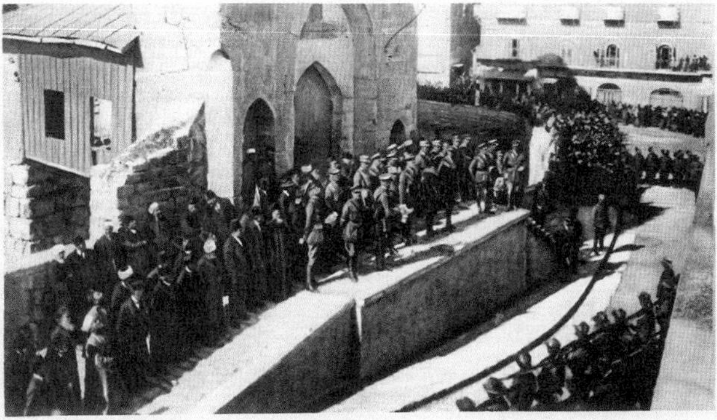

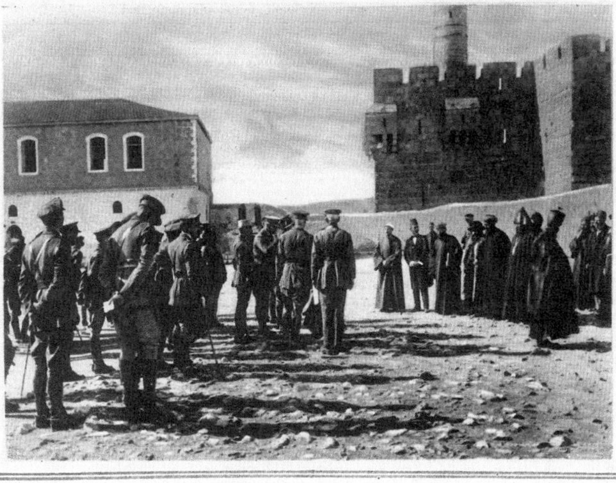

1. "AT THE BASE OF THE TOWER OF DAVID, STANDING WHEN CHRIST WAS IN JERUSALEM": A BRITISH OFFICER READING THE PROCLAMATION.
2. "GENERAL ALLENBY RECEIVED THE HEADS OF THE RELIGIOUS COMMUNITIES": IN THE BARRACK SQUARE AFTER THE PROCLAMATION.

"The Commander-in-Chief," writes Mr. W. T. Massey, who saw the Allied entry into Jerusalem, "had on his right the commander of the French detachment, and on his left the commander of the Italian detachment. The Italian, French, and American Military Attachés followed. . . . On the steps, at the base of the Tower of David, which was standing when Christ was in Jerusalem, the Proclamation of Military Law was read. . . . Re-forming, the procession moved up Zion Street to the barrack square, where General Allenby received the notables and the heads of the religious communities. The Mayor and the Mufti were presented, likewise the sheikhs in charge of the Mosques of Omar and Aksa, and Moslems. The Patriarchs of the Latin, Greek Orthodox, and Armenian Churches, and the Coptic Bishop, had been directed by the Turks to leave Jerusalem, but their representatives were introduced to General Allenby, also the heads of the Jewish Committees, Syrian Church, Greek Catholic Church, the Abyssinian Bishop, and a representative of the Anglican Church.

The War Illustrated, 4th January, 1919. Page 346

Pomp and Pride of Victory in East and West

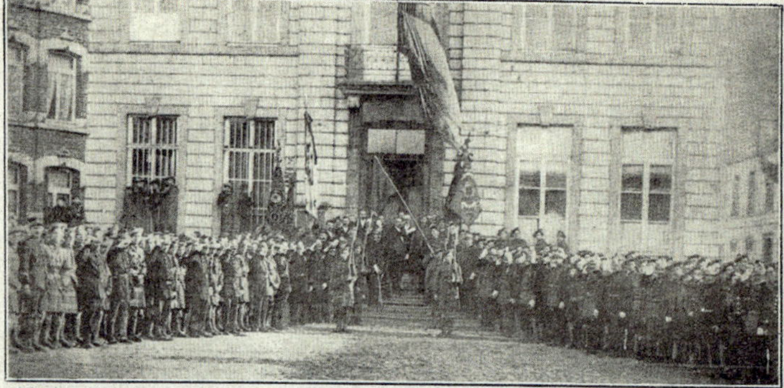

Fifth Gordon Highlanders presenting a regimental flag to the Mayor of Chievres to commemorate the entry of the British troops. Chievres, about twelve miles from Mons, was one of the last places occupied by the British Army before hostilities ceased on Nov. 11th, 1918.

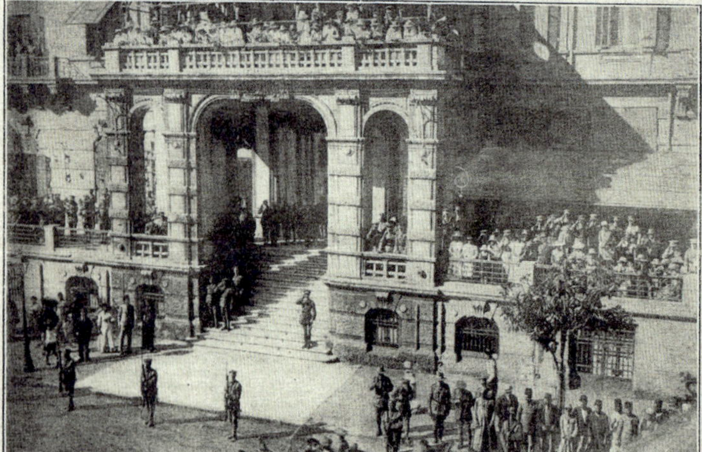

General Sir Edmund and Lady Allenby passing General Headquarters at Savoy Hotel, Cairo, when the conqueror of Jerusalem visited Cairo as the guest of the Sultan of Egypt, and was given a magnificent reception by the people.

JERUSALEM DELIVERED : *THANKSGIVING SERVICES IN LONDON.*

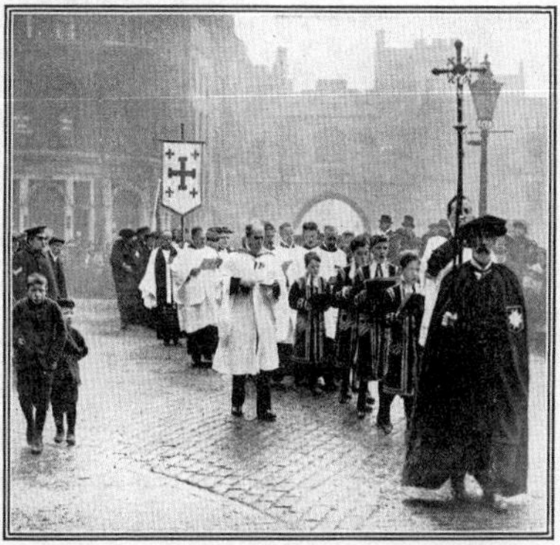

The Solemn Thanksgiving of the Order of St. John of Jerusalem

On January 11 the knights, members, and associates of the Order of the Hospital of St. John of Jerusalem in England attended a service of thanksgiving for the taking of the Holy City. The service was held in the Grand Priory Church, St. John's Square, Clerkenwell, the preacher being the Archbishop of York, the prelate of the order, who took for his text, "If I forget thee, O Jerusalem, let my right hand forget her cunning" (Psalm cxxxvii., 5). The procession is here seen on its way from St. John's Gate to the Priory Church

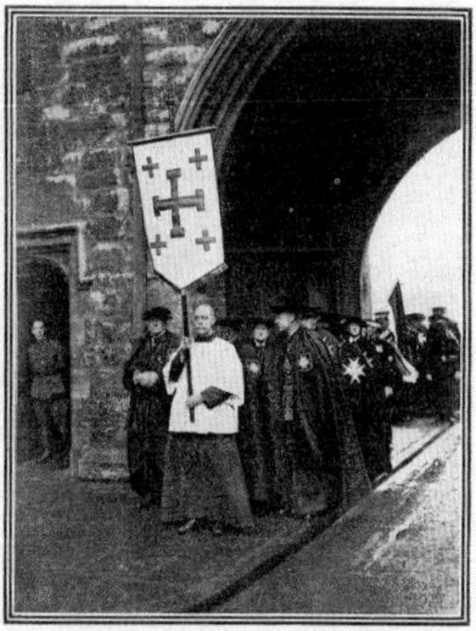

The Procession Passing under St. John's Gateway

The Hospital of St. John of Jerusalem in England was founded by one Jordan Briset in 1100, and in 1185 the buildings of the order were dedicated by Heraclius, Patriarch of Jerusalem, to the furtherance of the Holy Crusade. Little remains of the magnificent priory except the gateway shown above, from which for centuries the knights of the order set out on their journeys to the Holy Land

A special service of thanksgiving for the recapture of Jerusalem from the hands of the Turk was held on January 11 by the Order of St. John of Jerusalem in England at St. John's Priory Church, Clerkenwell, the King being represented by Lord Sandhurst. A procession of the knights in their black silk mantles, embroidered with the white Maltese Cross and English lions, and black velvet Tudor hats, was formed at St. John's Gate, and proceeded to the church with the banner of the Kingdom of Jerusalem at their head. It was in the first year of the reign of Henry I. that the building of the English home of the order was begun, and before many years had elapsed it was acknowledged as the richest and most powerful priory in Christendom. Fifty years later some three hundred of the Knights Hospitallers of St. John, led by Theodric, their prior, passed under the gateway on their way to the Holy Land. "They marched with the banner of St. John proudly unfurled before them, and as they passed over London Bridge, saluted, with hood in hand, the crowds congregated to see their departure, recommending themselves and their cause to the prayers of the people."

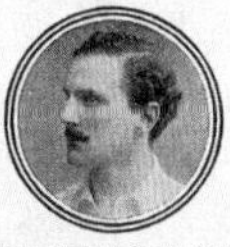

Lieut.-Colonel R. Storrs, C.M.G.

Who has been appointed Military Governor of Jerusalem

The Knights of St. John continued to grow in power and riches until the rebellion of Wat Tyler in 1381, which had the most disastrous consequences for the order, for the mob attacked and burned the great priory, and the prior, "a most valiant knight," was afterwards beheaded on Tower Hill. The priory was rebuilt, only to be destroyed again in the reign of Edward VI. In the words of the chronicler, it "was barbarously blown up with gunpowder, and the stones carried to finish the Protector Somerset's house in the Strand. But strange judgments fell upon him afterwards." Of all the magnificent buildings almost the only relic left is the great gateway shown in the accompanying illustrations. The procession passed to the Priory Church, which is built on, or rather just to the east of, the site of the original building, which was circular, in imitation of the Church of the Holy Sepulchre at Jerusalem. This circular site is still indicated on the roadway, but the only traces of the older church are found in the crypt, which still survives under the present building. St. John's Gate forms a very real link between London and the Holy Land.

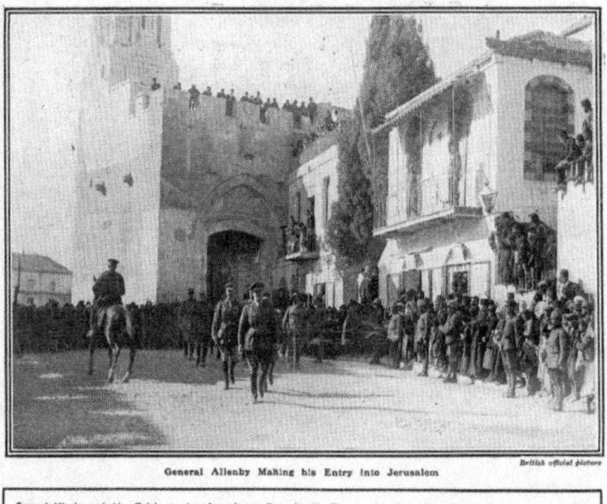

British official picture

General Allenby Making his Entry into Jerusalem

General Allenby made his official entry into Jerusalem on December 11. He entered on foot, and at the Jaffa Gate he was received by a detachment of guards representative of the troops which had taken part in the fighting in Palestine

To the inhabitants of Jerusalem the Blessed and the people dwelling in its vicinity.

I here and now proclaim it to be under Martial Law, under which form of administration it will remain so long as military considerations make it necessary.

However, lest any of you should be alarmed by reason of your experience at the hands of the enemy, who has retired, I hereby inform you that it is my desire that every person should pursue his lawful business without fear of interruption. Furthermore, since your city is regarded with affection by the adherents of three of the great religions of mankind, and its soil has been consecrated by the prayers and pilgrimages of multitudes of devout people of these three religions for many centuries, therefore do I make known to you that every sacred building, monument, holy spot, shrine, traditional site, endowment, pious bequest, or customary place of prayer, of whatever form of the three religions, will be maintained and protected according to the existing customs and beliefs of those to whose faiths they are sacred.

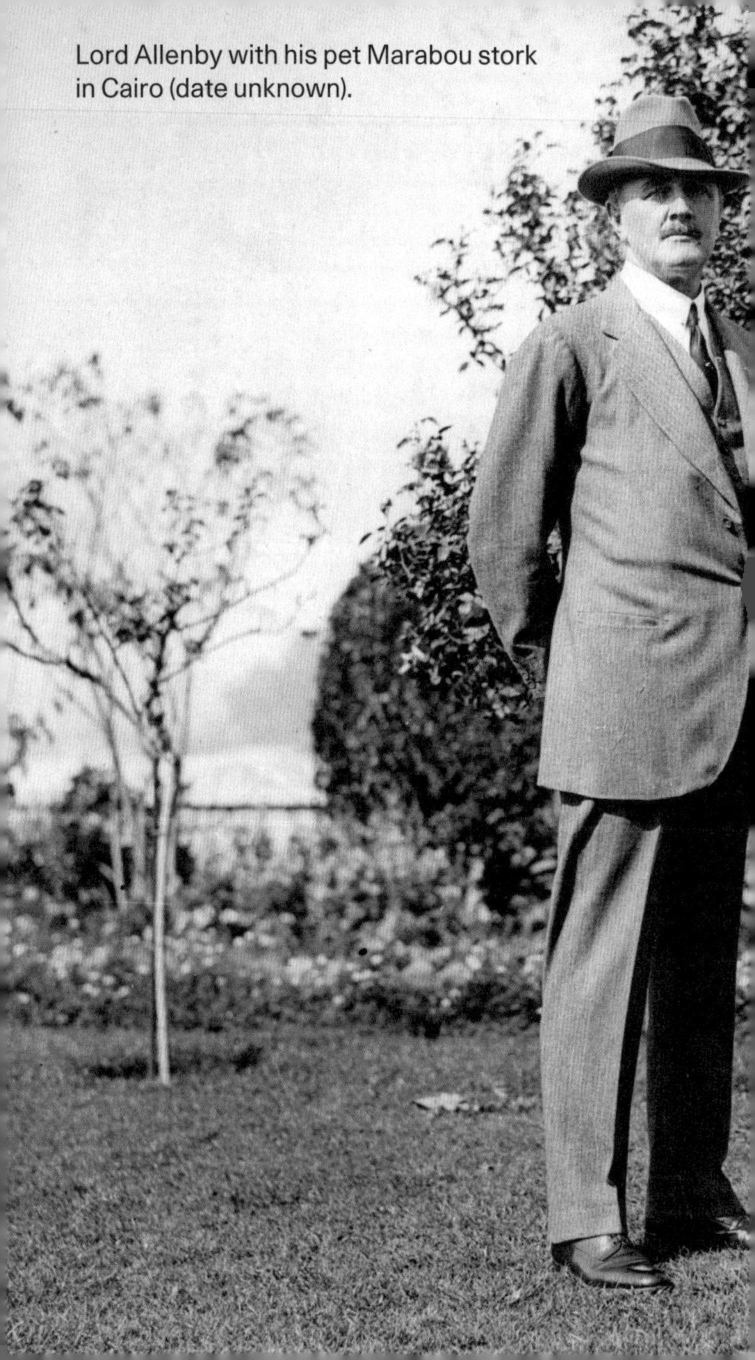

Lord Allenby with his pet Marabou stork in Cairo (date unknown).

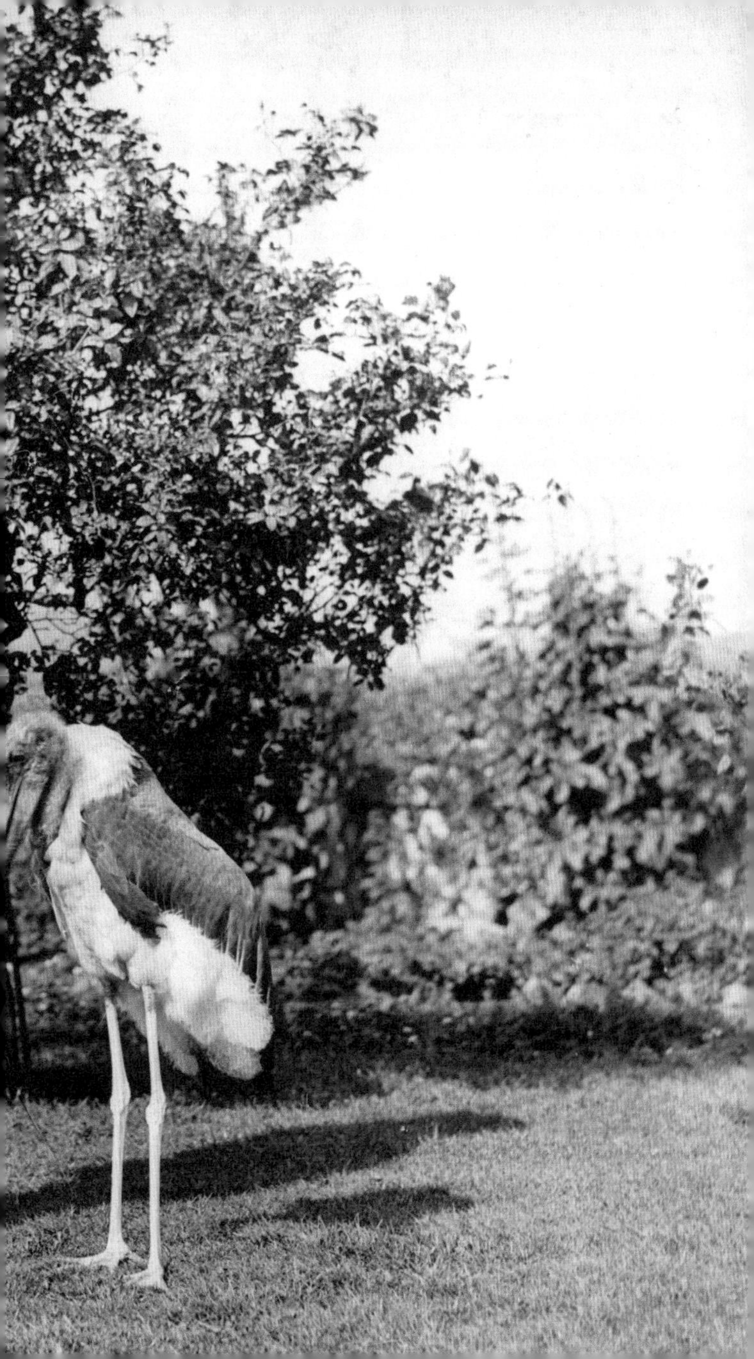

Stills from *Lord Allenby in Cairo*, 1922.

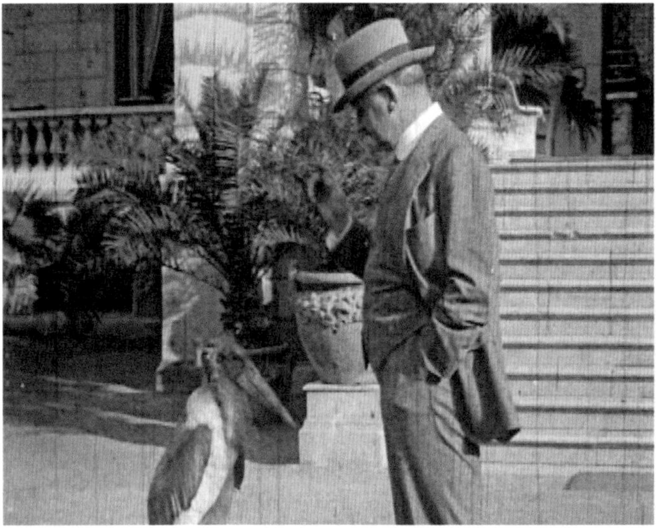

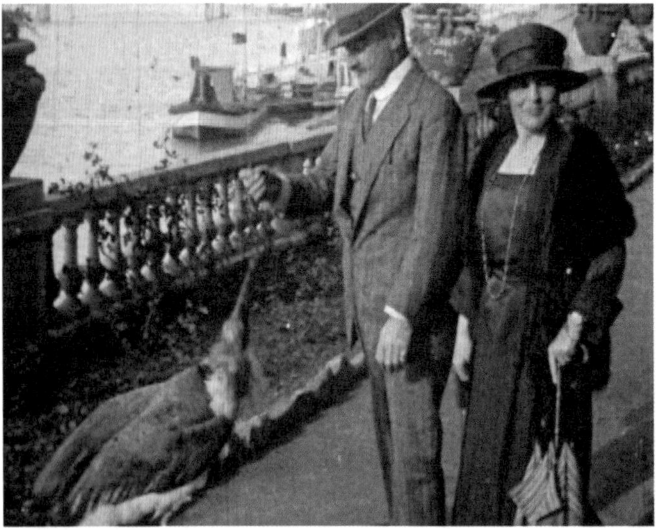

Clipping from unknown newspaper sent to the artist in 2016.

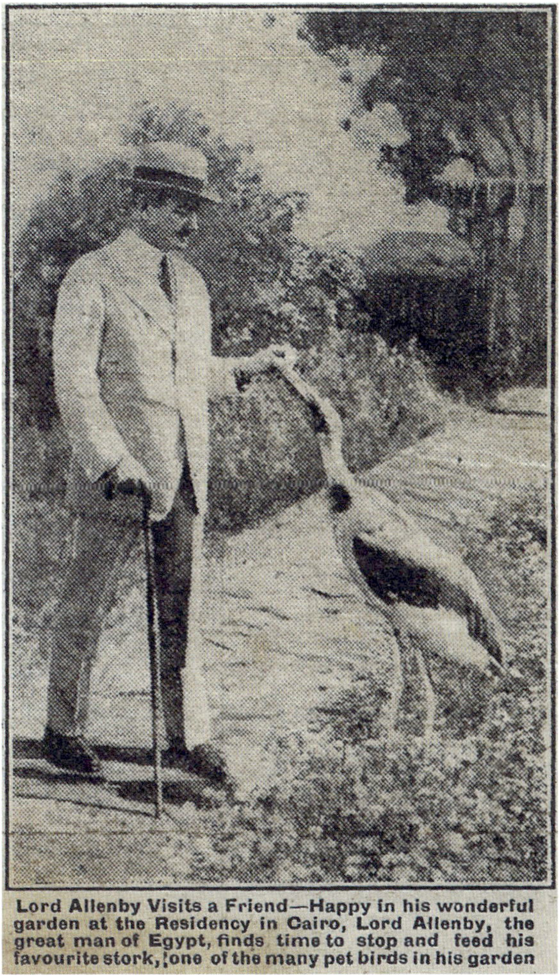

Lord Allenby Visits a Friend—Happy in his wonderful garden at the Residency in Cairo, Lord Allenby, the great man of Egypt, finds time to stop and feed his favourite stork, one of the many pet birds in his garden

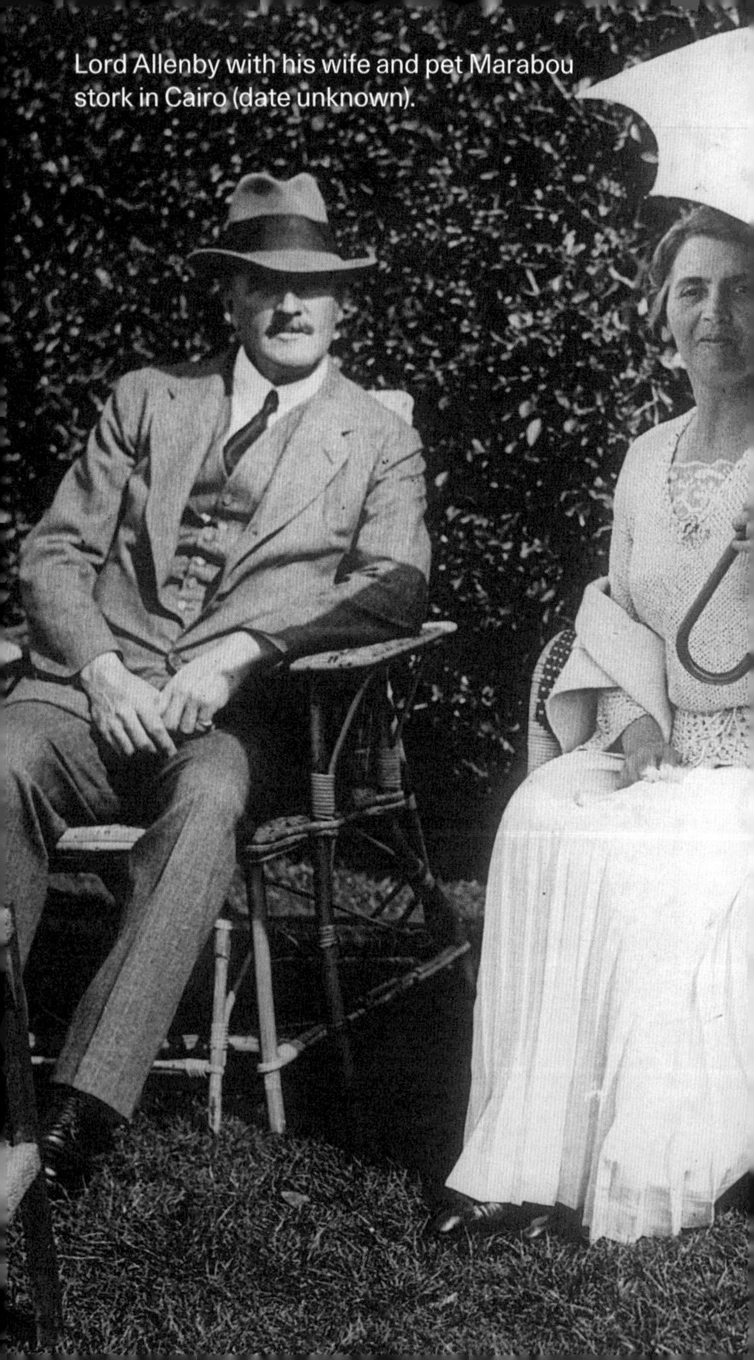

Lord Allenby with his wife and pet Marabou stork in Cairo (date unknown).

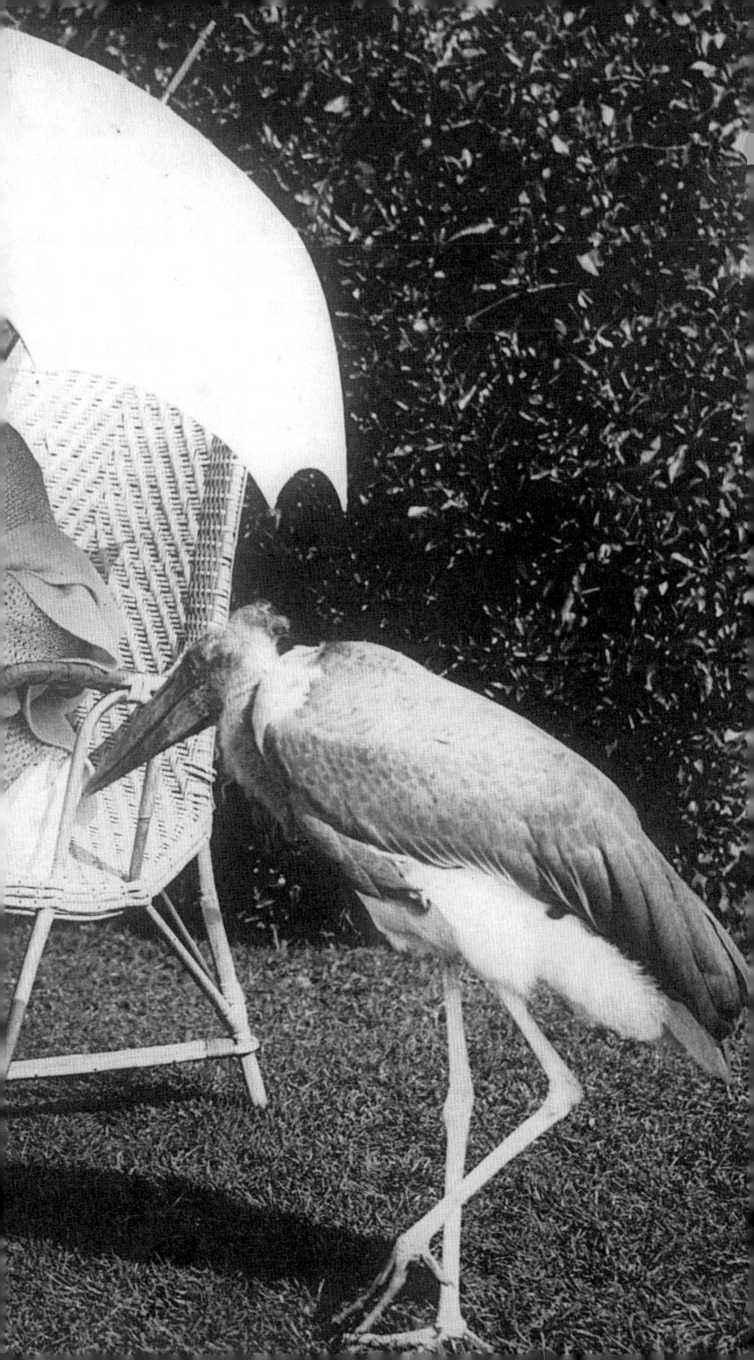

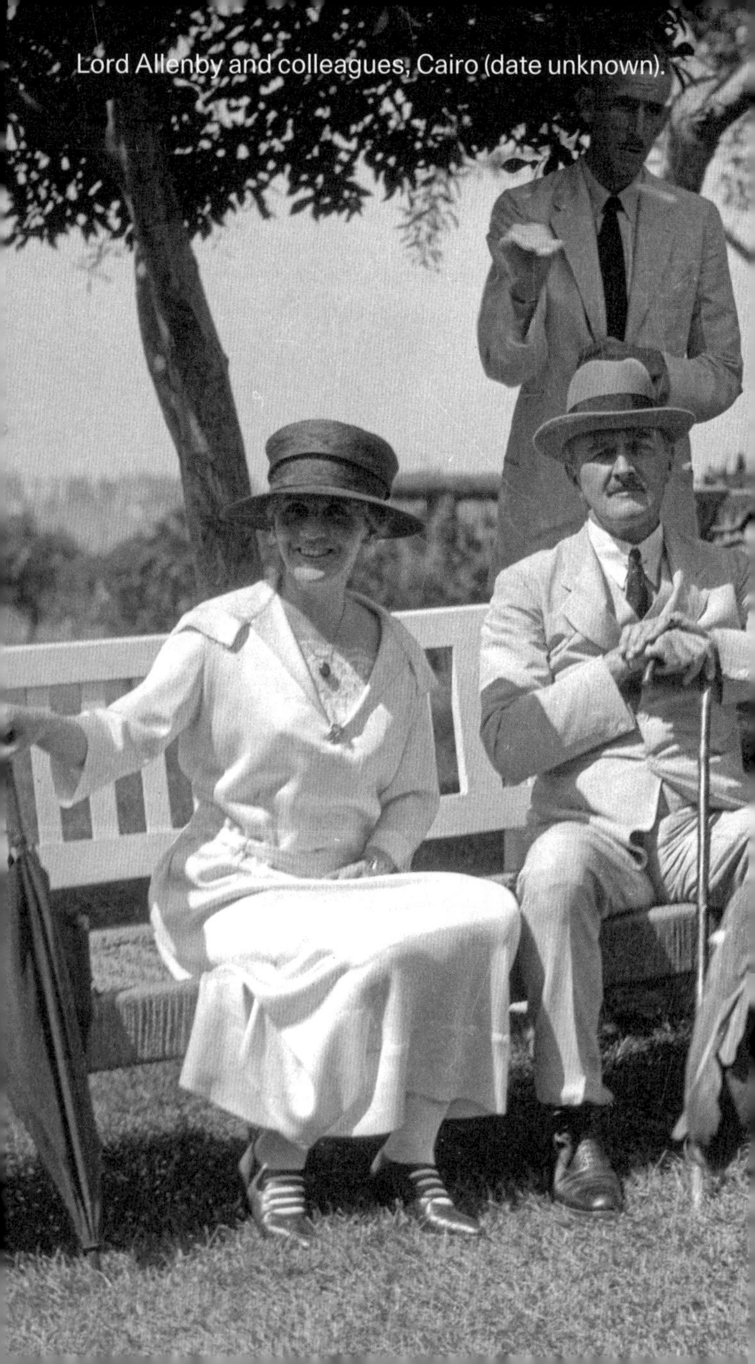

Lord Allenby and colleagues, Cairo (date unknown).

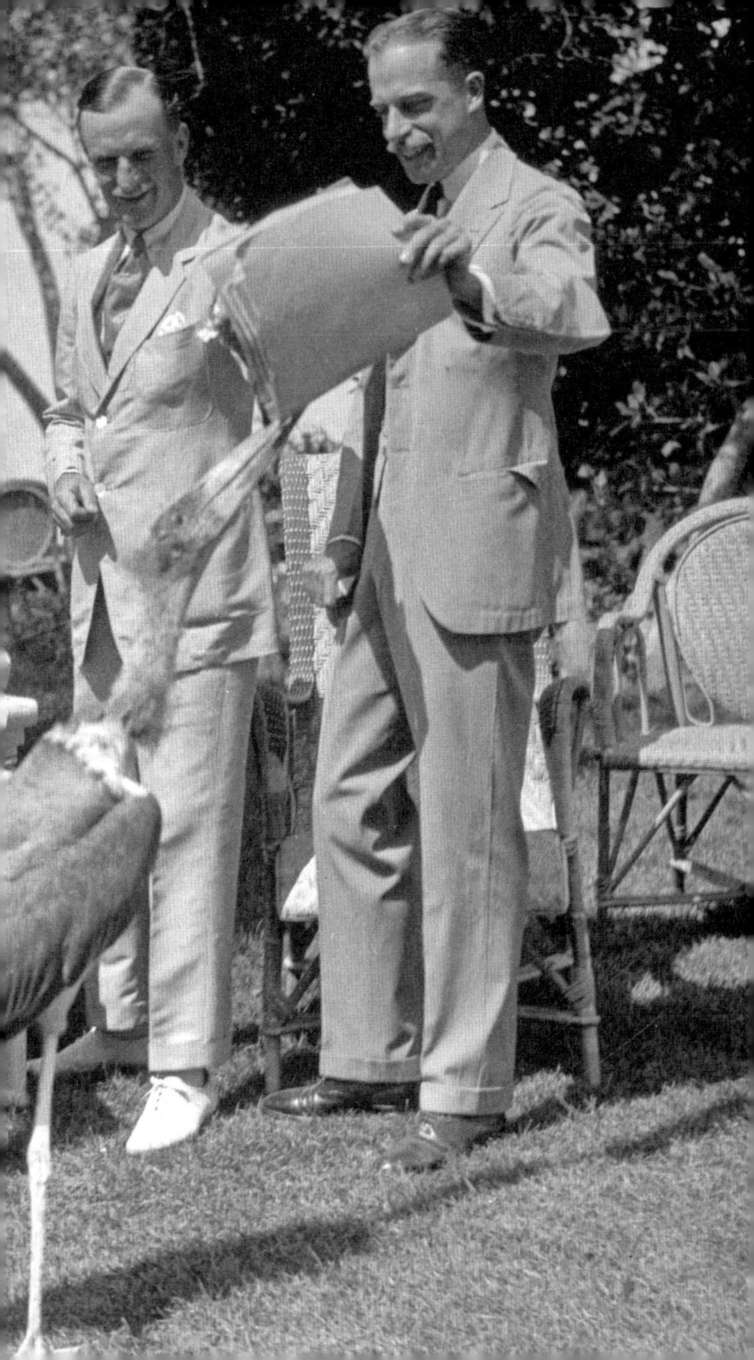

Which Reality Do You Want?

Heba Y. Amin in conversation with Adam Harvey

Heba Y. Amin How do you feel about spy birds?

Adam Harvey Well, I'm not as surprised as you think I might be because I can see the utilitarian value in spy-technology-equipped animals for reconnaissance. I think it's the absurdity of the detainment protocols that make it appear more circus-like. From a national-security perspective, this might not be what you expected me to say, and perhaps it's a less popular response, but feathered espionage is far less shocking than the types of spying happening today. Everyone's a spy and everyone's a forensic analyst. And it's only weird if you're not getting paid for it. From this perspective, my only question is why use a bird instead of a cat?

HYA Yes, like the CIA's Operation Acoustic Kitty from the 1960s.[1] I discovered a recent project about crows. The US military–funded research program looked into using networks of "spy crows" to locate soldiers missing in action. The researchers extended the work to see if birds might help them find Osama bin Laden. They were also interested in the research of John Marzluff, a wildlife biologist, who explored whether or not crows are capable of face recognition. We often think of using animals for reconnaissance and surveillance as an old-fashioned strategy since today they are replaced by more advanced technologies.

AH In the recent history of the world, there are probably many instances of animal involvement in spy operations that we don't know about, but hopefully the government files on these will be declassified soon. Training crows for facial recognition is both unusual and relatively normal. Dogs are routinely used to sniff out bombs and for other military purposes, and you could say dogs have been militarized or weaponized, but this expression is overused because virtually everything is either militarized or is linked to militaristic origins. For example, horses are used for policing. Mice have been irradiated during nuclear weapons testing. There is a parallel dark military world that we won't fully understand for another fifty years when files have been declassified. Documents showing the CIA's early involvement funding face-recognition studies in the early 1960s were only declassified a few years ago. The perplexity of spy birds, along with any other spy tech, can only be partially understood in the present. This temporary blindness makes it somewhat impossible to know whether something is an anomaly or part of a larger historical trend. Eventually these spy technologies slowly trickle into the consumer world. A lot of my work is about understanding and defending against the normalization of defense technologies. Facial recognition, for example, is used a lot right now because of access to free application programming interfaces and open-source code—and it's typically code that people reuse when building their own software—that's not much different from what government agencies use. Amazon's Rekognition provides the same technology to law enforcement agencies as it does to consumers looking to recognize celebrities in photos and videos. It's just available to a different database of people. You could say that this gives everyone access to law enforcement grade technology, but actually it's the other way around. Law enforcement agencies have access to consumer grade technology. It's that good. Gregory C. Allen, a fellow at Center for a New American Security, says: "There is no super secret government lab with advanced AI way better than commercial industry. The government, the military, they are behind commercial industry."[2] This flips the previous logic that military technology flows from defense departments down to consumers. Now it flows in reverse. Military grade just means full access to Facebook, Twitter, and Google. To me, that is even more shocking than the bird story.

HYA I think what is frightening is how pervasive such technologies are in our daily lives, and yet we're all knowingly participating in it.

AH I don't think Western society fully understands how these companies have monopolized society. Just imagine if Facebook, Twitter, Amazon, and Google all permanently deactivated your online accounts right now. It's not a fun thought.

HYA I suppose this is also why I am fascinated by the story of the bird. It highlights a system that a lot of people don't want to admit they are participating in.

AH National security creates fear and that stifles discourse, but it's healthy to debate these topics because they're weird and a large part of the world in which we live. I think it's easier to talk about these issues now. It was much more difficult in the years following 9/11. Discussing face recognition and face detection, for example, were considered potential indicators of terrorist behavior in the United States. People were really paranoid. The FBI even posted a terror-alert notice that warned US citizens to watch out for people paying with cash. That's what cash is for. To pay for things!

HYA Many people around the world are considered suspects, and are, in fact, treated as such. Part of my research for this project is to look at the ways in which photography and its representation of particular geographies utilize the language of occupation and colonization in the visualization of landscape, particularly through the technologies of warfare. The early usage of aerial photography, especially in the early twentieth century, had to do with reconnaissance. Seeing the world from above introduced a new perspective of territory that played into the hands of colonial ideology—it visualized new lands for the purpose of expansion. More recent developments in drone imaging and technology allow for further control over populations through the visual tracking of their movement. In a presentation you made, you stated that you stopped being a photographer because you felt discomfort in the way photography exerts control over other people. Does your work now attempt to reverse those hierarchies? How do you address that vision of the aerial gaze?

AH At first, I thought photography was art. Then I realized it is mostly surveillance and not too different from aerial imaging. I found this problematic and boring. Photographing people who did not want to be photographed wasn't fun. Experiencing this too many times, I was inspired to create countersurveillance interventions. Photography is actually quite aggressive and, of course, Susan Sontag was influential in thinking about this. This problem with photography became more acute when everyone started posting and sharing photos online in the early 2000s. Not only were people unable to control a photographer's initial capture, but were essentially being rephotographed as their images were copied around the internet. Working as a programmer at the time, I understood that the photos could not easily be removed from the internet. I also understood that face-recognition technology was growing and going to become more ubiquitous. The consequence being that all of the photos posted in the early 2000s would eventually be analyzed with face-recognition technology. And that's exactly what's happening today. Many of these online photos are now being used as training data for artificial intelligence. This is the focus of a new research project I've started called "MegaPixels," which looks at the problem of information supply chains that fuel facial-recognition technologies. As Geoffrey Hinton has said: "Our relationship to computers has changed. Instead of programming them, we now show them and they figure it out."[3] In other words, the data that comes from party photos taken in the early 2000s, for example, is now being used to program neural networks.

HYA Where do you envision this taking us?

AH I think there will be more legislation. But I'm not sure how effective it will be because the concept of face recognition is not yet standardized and doesn't work that well. Is a face 20 × 20 pixels or 1 megapixel? Without enough data, it's not possible to actually recognize faces in a large data set. Face recognition is a probabilistic determination. It's not absolute. Phone numbers are absolute, and you can be sure if you dialed the right person or not. Facial recognition doesn't work like that.

HYA Why not?

AH Facial recognition usually means doing a similarity search with increasing amounts of accuracy as you gather more resolution. The three ways you gather resolution are through: 1) the sampling resolution (which would be pixels per square inch); 2) the time domain (gathering it over time, which would mean annual enrollment for a biometric passport); and 3) spectral sampling (the sensor's bandwidth). At a high enough resolution, you also get iris recognition, or even detect skin cancer. IBM has been working on that. From a 100 × 100–pixel image of a face, you can also read heart rate, breathing rate, and pupil dilation.

HYA In the past, your work has dealt with evading these kinds of technologies, as with "CV Dazzle," a project where you used fashion and makeup to camouflage the face so it is unrecognizable to a computer, or "Stealth Wear," a range of anti-drone clothing created to hide the wearer from heat-detection technologies. With these new directions of technological research you're describing, how does invisibility work in these new contexts? How can people hide when camouflaging oneself becomes increasingly difficult?

AH The camouflage equation has changed. It's no longer a good idea to use camouflage until you really need it, because all online images can be used as training data. This is why I've become interested in information supply chains. You can't build a face-recognition system if you don't have enough data. This has been a problem for Microsoft recently: they said they couldn't sell face-recognition software to a law enforcement agency in California because they didn't have enough data to detect different skin tones and facial structures. That's because they train mostly using photos of white males taken from the internet. This situation highlights the value of data for any data-driven AI neural network product. You can't make it without a vast amount of data. So instead of thinking about conventional camouflage, I'm thinking about limiting supply chains as way to limit the scope of visibility.

HYA I've been looking at "bionic thinking" and these approaches to learning from nature and then transferring that knowledge to technology. Artificial intelligence becomes completely ubiquitous when we no longer know the difference between what is and isn't real. Drones are starting to look more and more like real birds. SmartBird from Festo is one example of a drone that can flap its wings like a herring gull. In 2011 a drone, which looked like the SmartBird, crashed in Chaman, Pakistan. Imagine the confusion of finding such an object in a place where people are so accustomed to drone attacks. What happens when we can no longer differentiate a machine from a living thing?

AH If you don't know the bird is a fake, you experience it as if it were real. From a distance, there's no sensorial difference, and it doesn't matter. I think about this every time I go to a restaurant and there are flowers on the table. If I don't touch the flowers, I can happily assume they're real. Which reality do you want? Maybe we'll appreciate things less because we can't tell if they're real or not, and we'll have to assume that all the restaurant flowers are fake. I think it means living in a world where we never really know where reality ends and illusion begins. It's like we're floating in space without the enjoyment of floating.

1 In the 1960s, the CIA intended to use cats to spy on the Kremlin and Soviet embassies. For a full account, see Emily Anthes, *Frankenstein's Cat: Cuddling Up to Biotech's Brave New Beasts* (New York: Farrar, Straus and Giroux, 2013).

2 See Gregory Allen, Gayle Lemmon, Ryan Tseng, and Hanne Tidnam, "Autonomy in Service," a16z Podcast, 2019, https://soundcloud.com/a16z/autonomy-service-national-security-ai.

3 See Gregory Hinton, interview with Deep Learning, *coursera*, https://www.coursera.org/lecture/neural-networks-deep-learning/geoffrey-hinton-interview-dcm5r.

Pages 140–51: Stills from Heba Y. Amin's *As Birds Flying* (2016). This short film uses found drone footage (including aerial views of savannas and wetlands, and Israeli settlements in Galilea) and audio sequences from the 1995 film *Birds of Darkness*, starring Adel Emam and directed by Sharif Arafah.

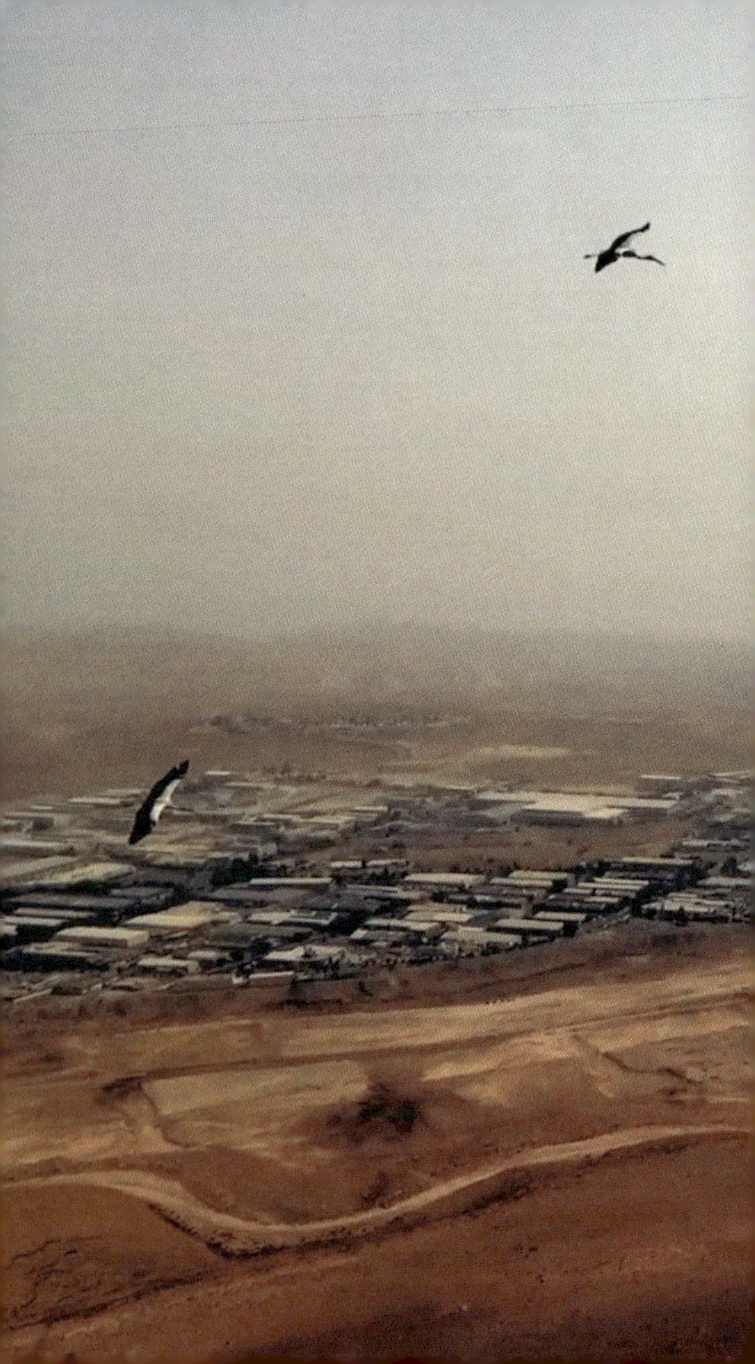

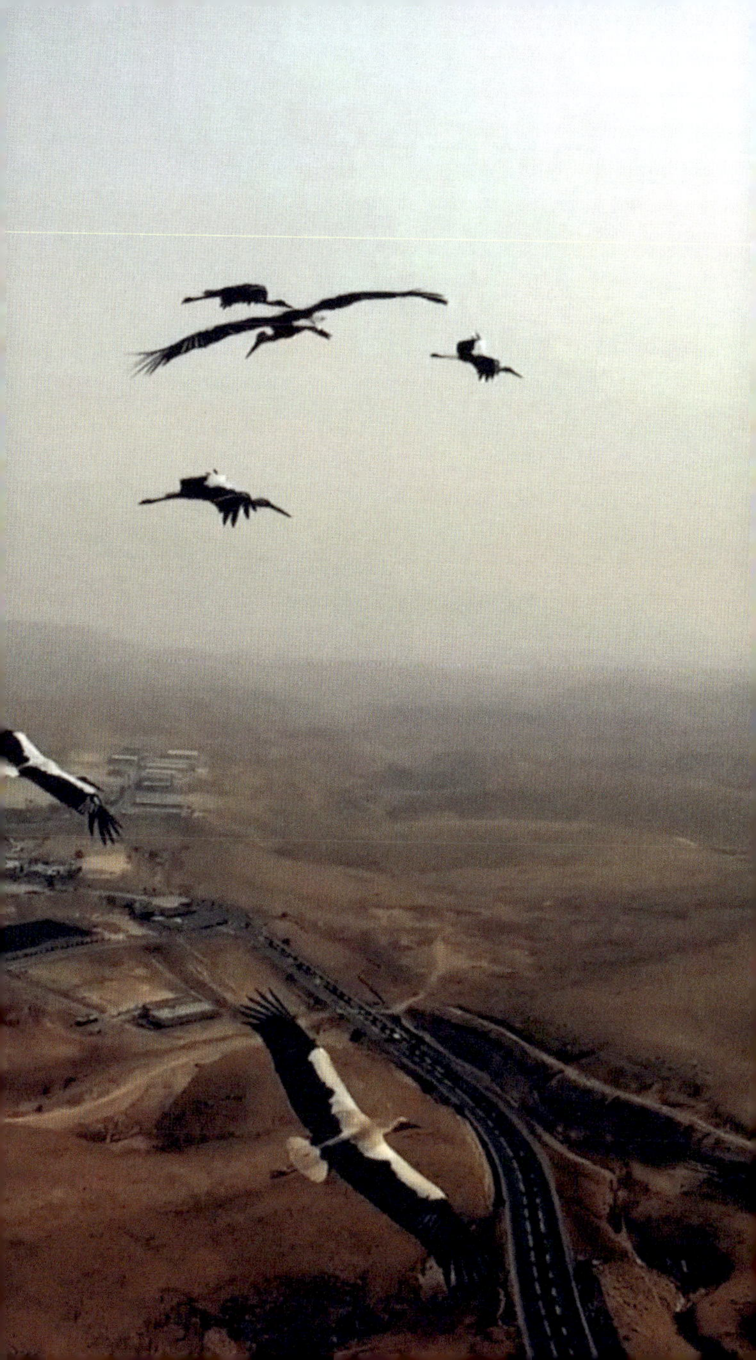

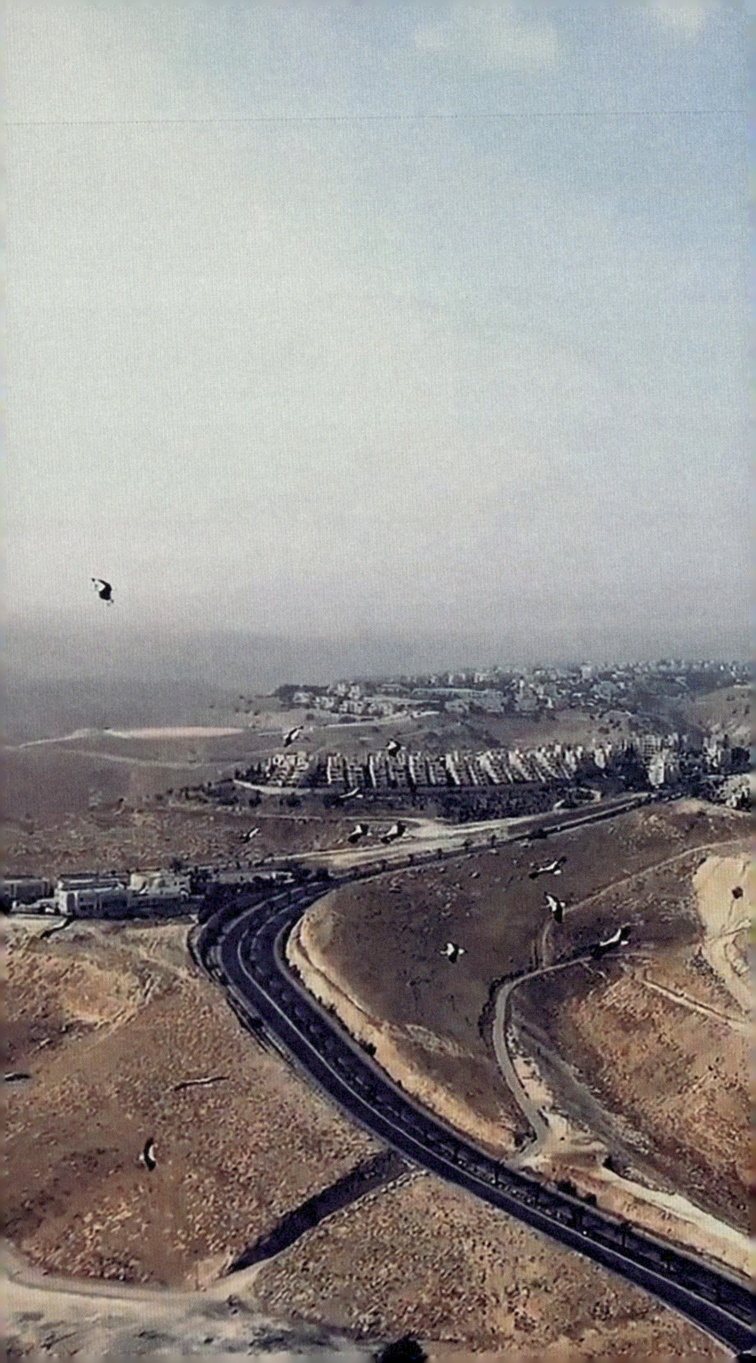

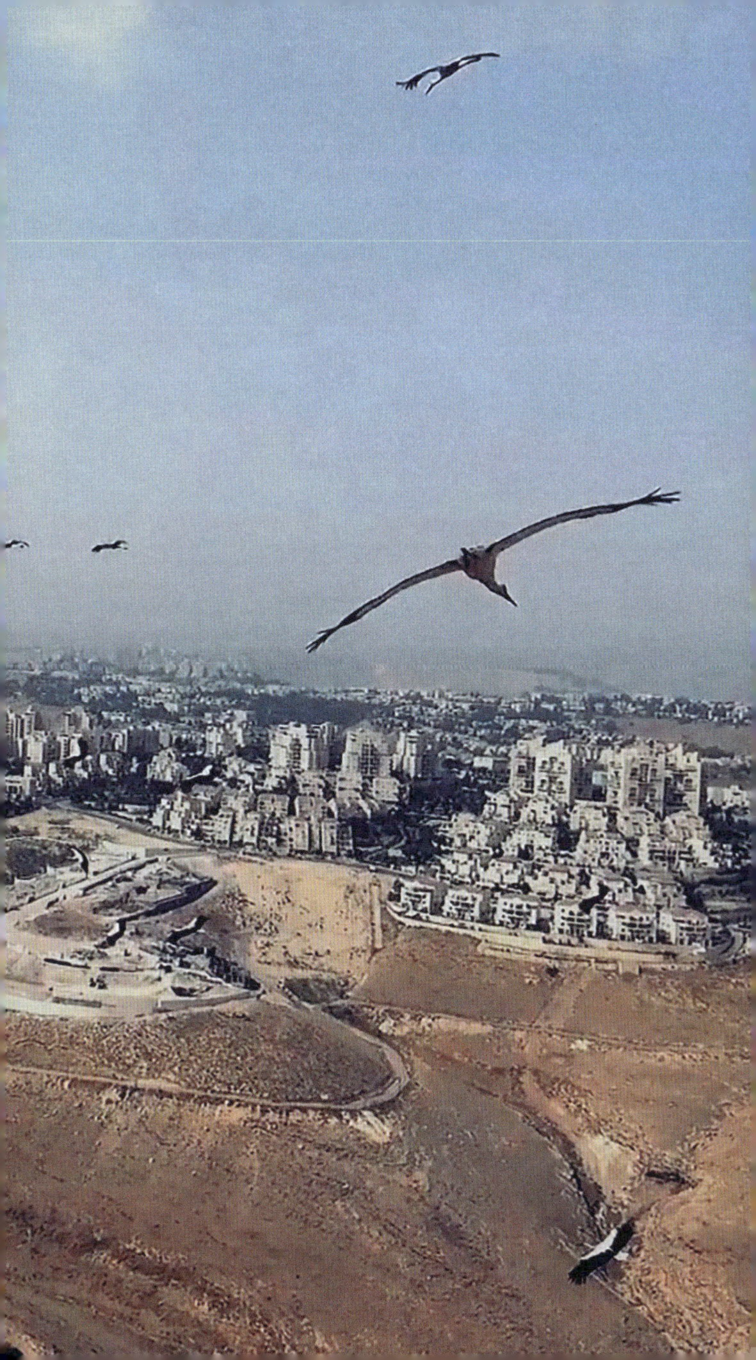

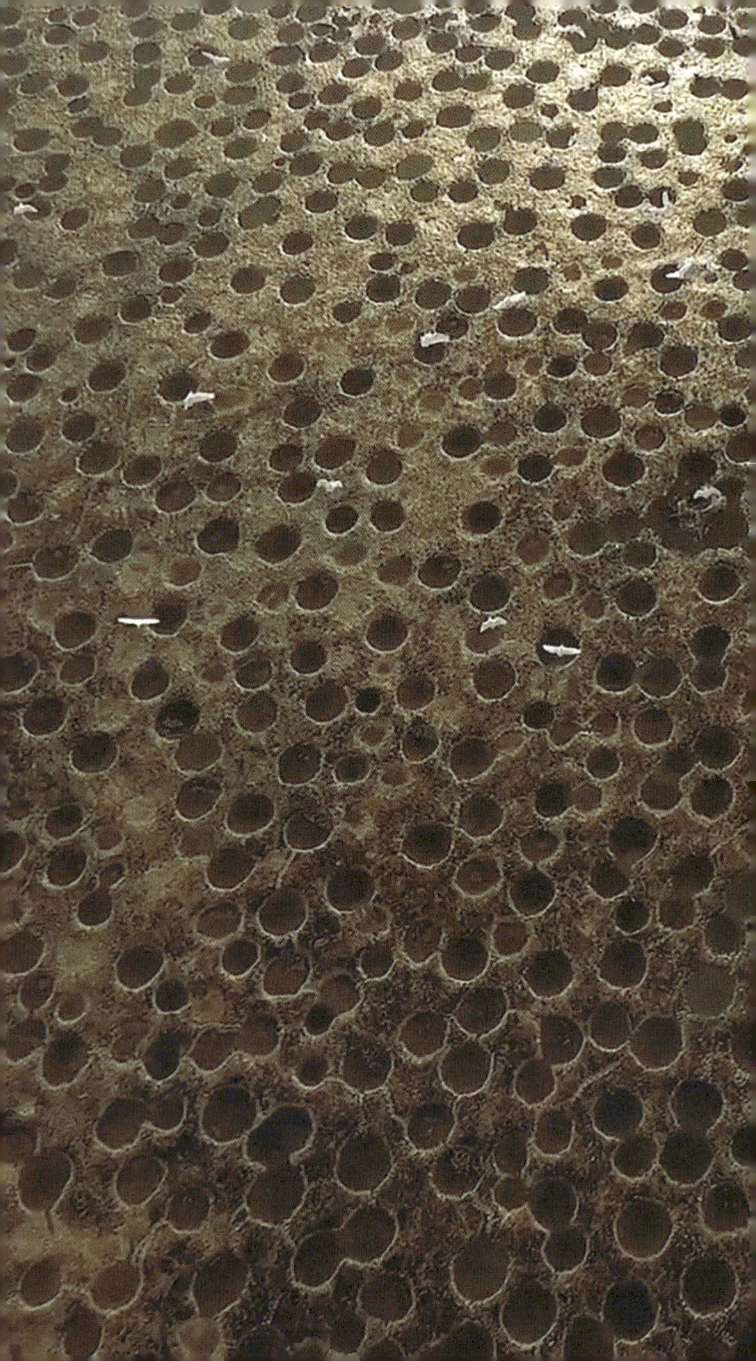

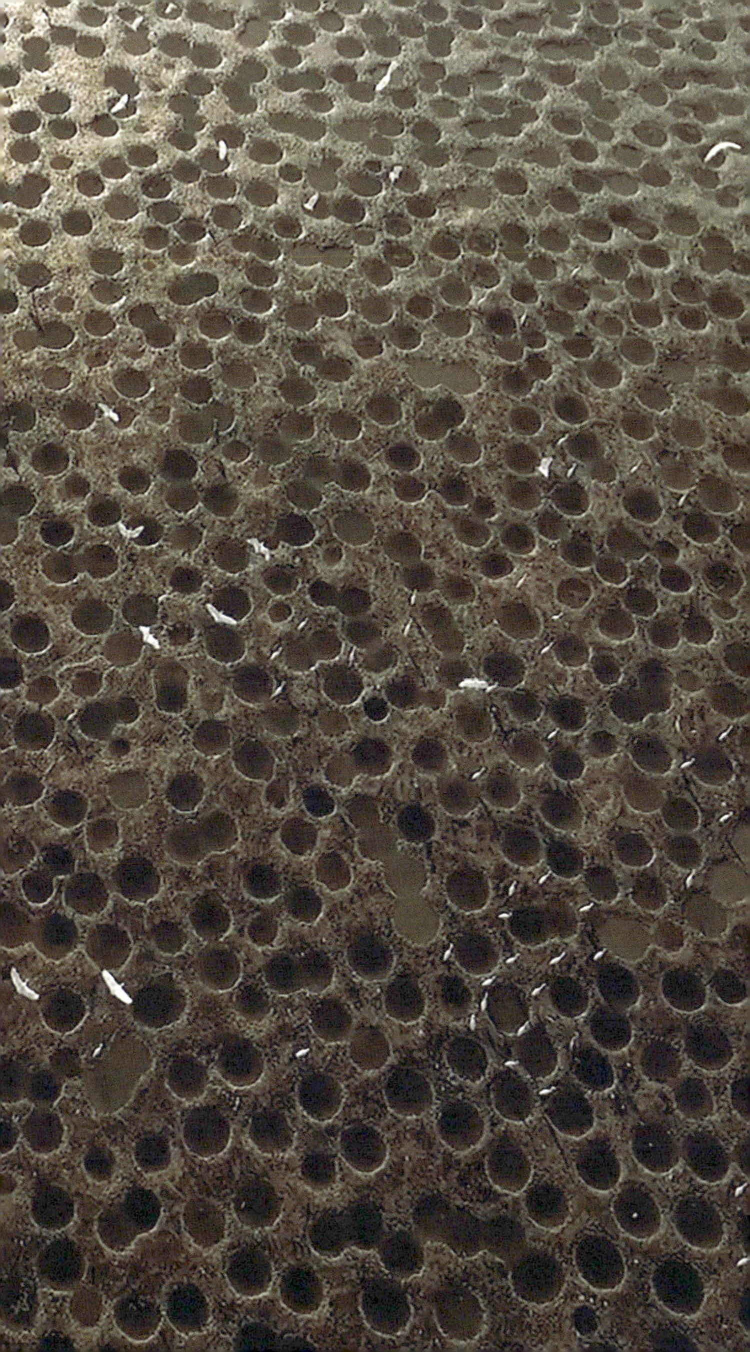

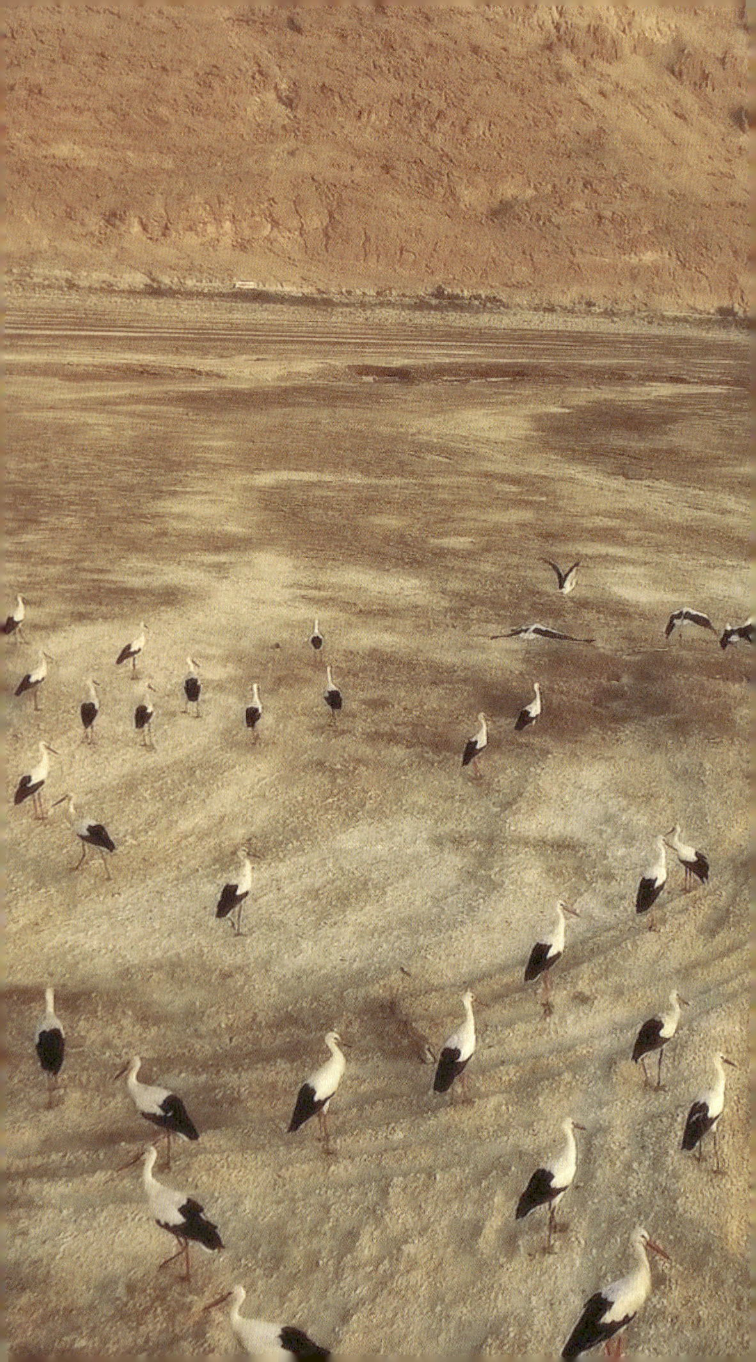

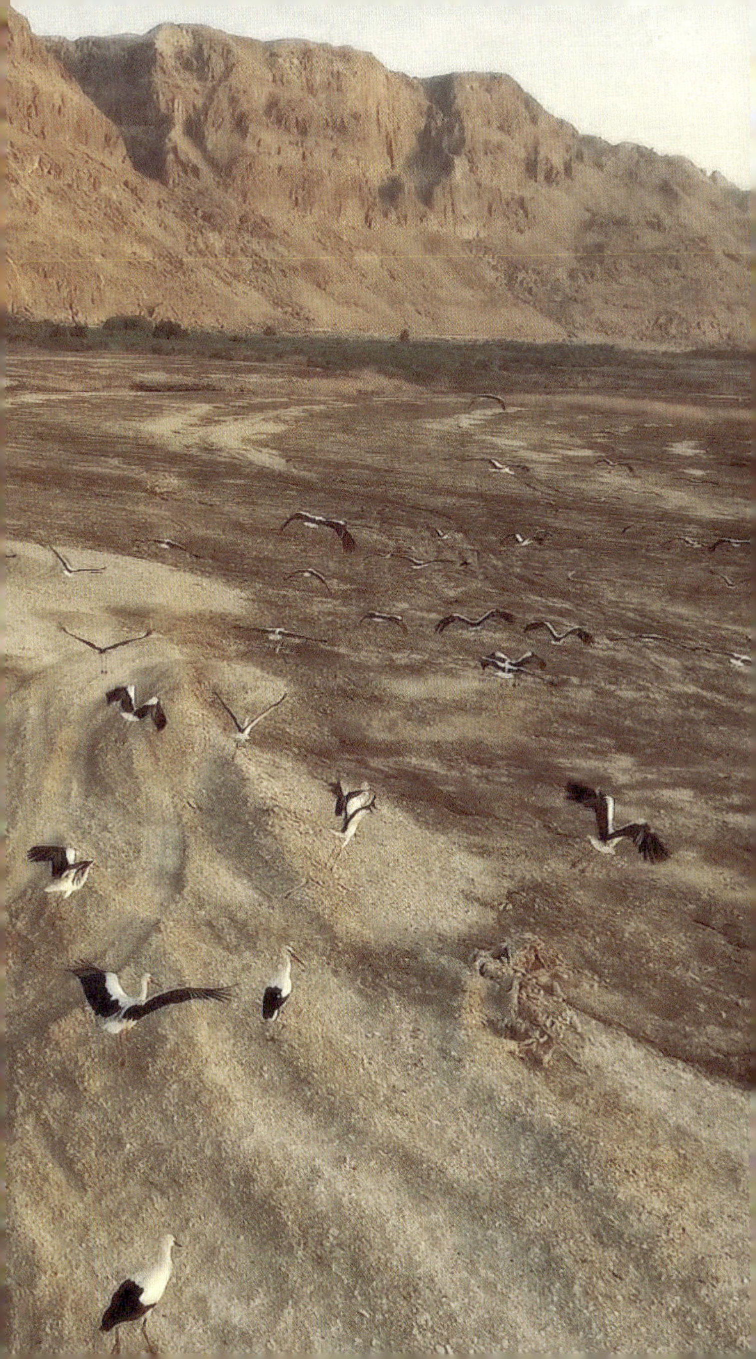

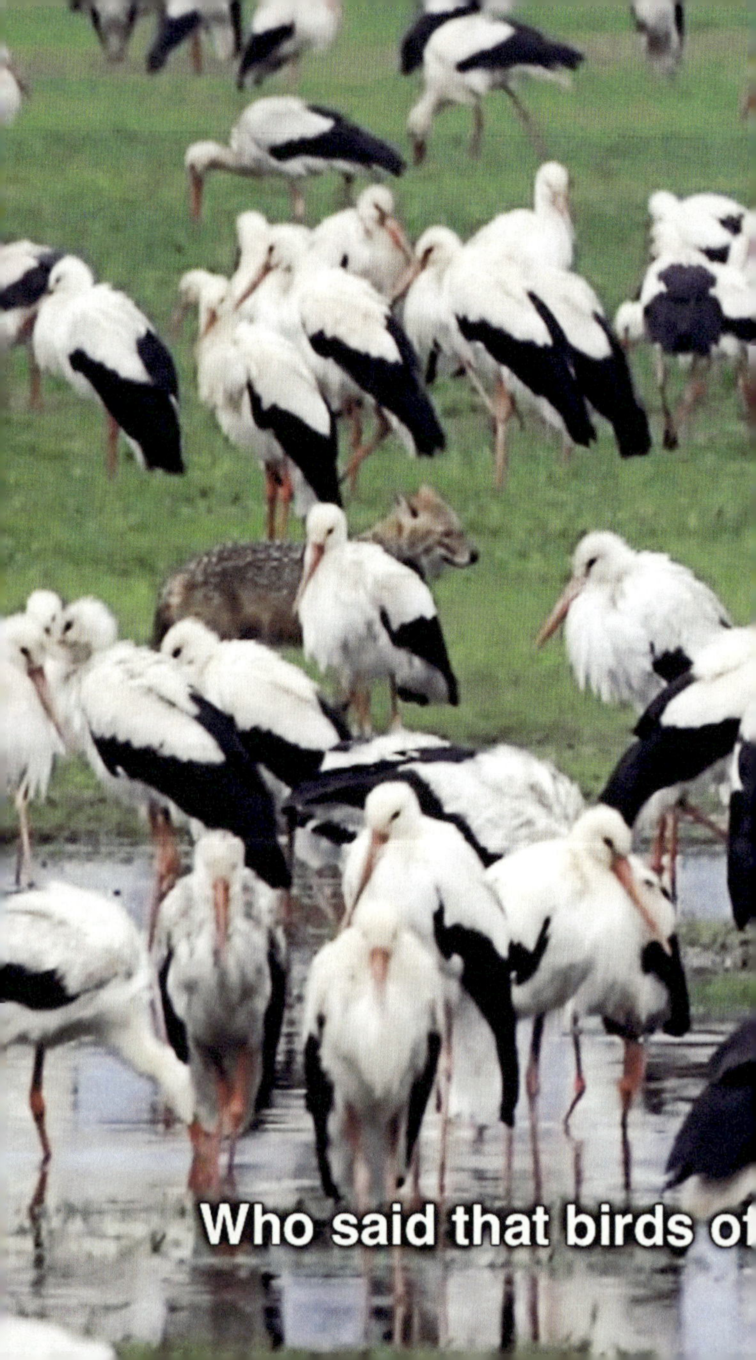
Who said that birds of

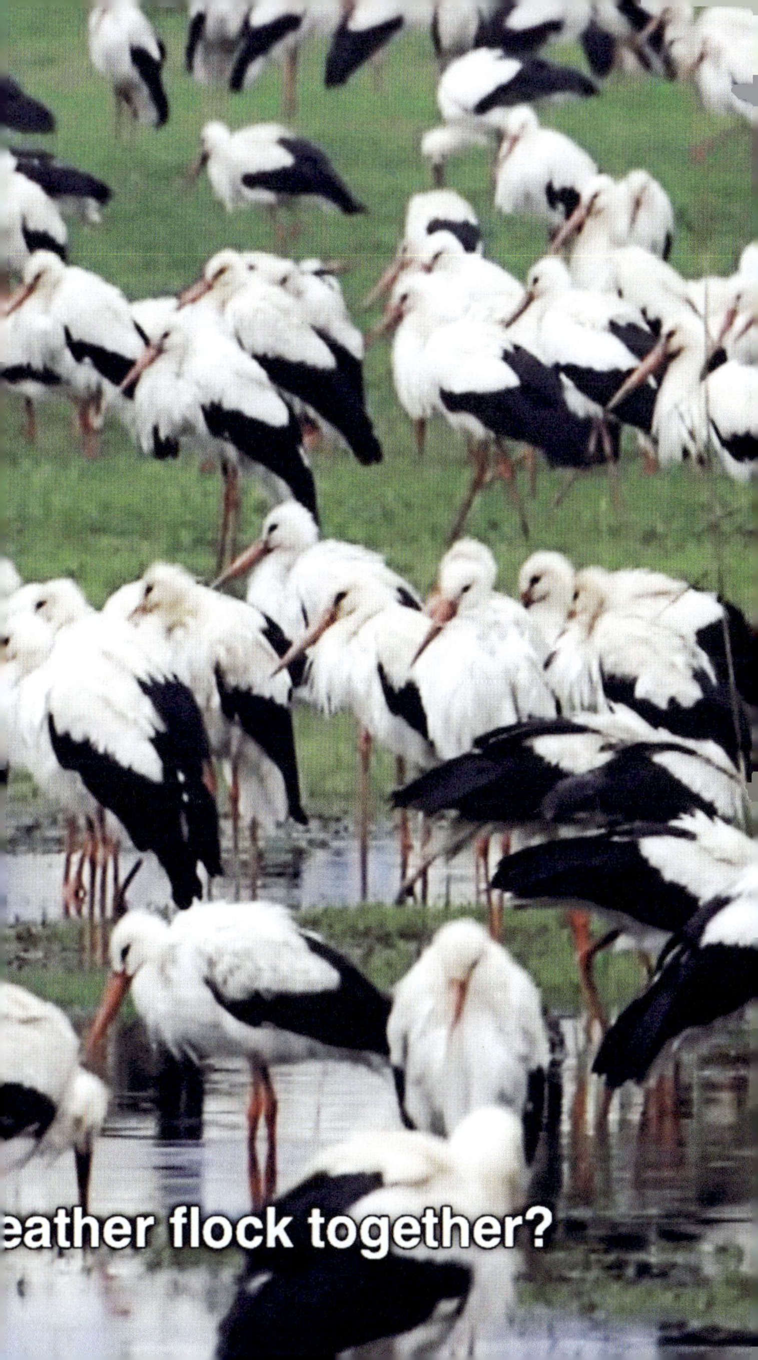
eather flock together?

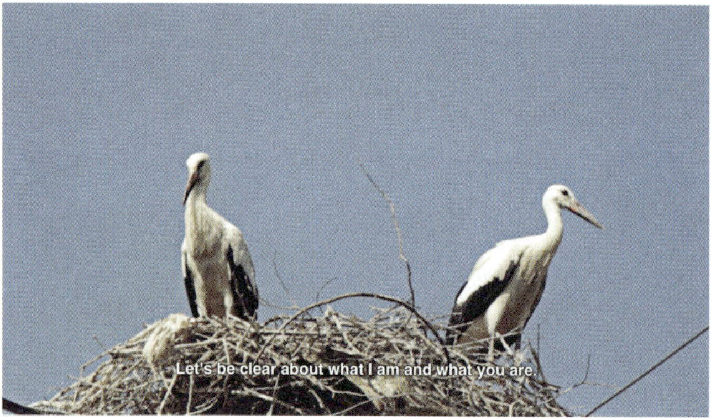
Let's be clear about what I am and what you are.

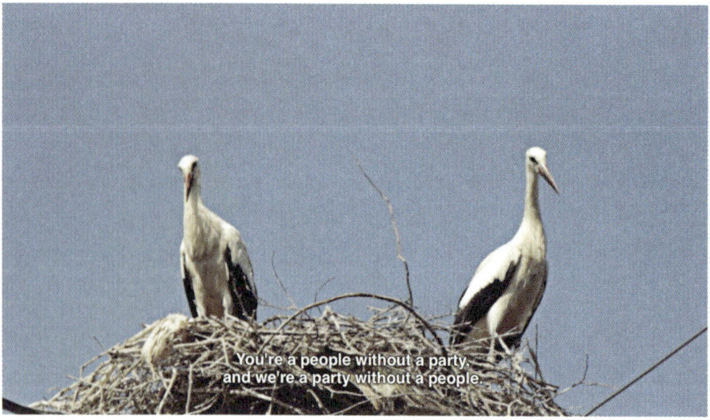
You're a people without a party,
and we're a party without a people.

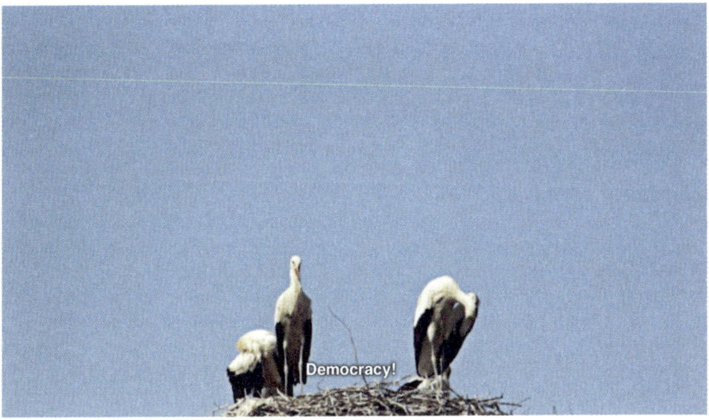
Democracy!

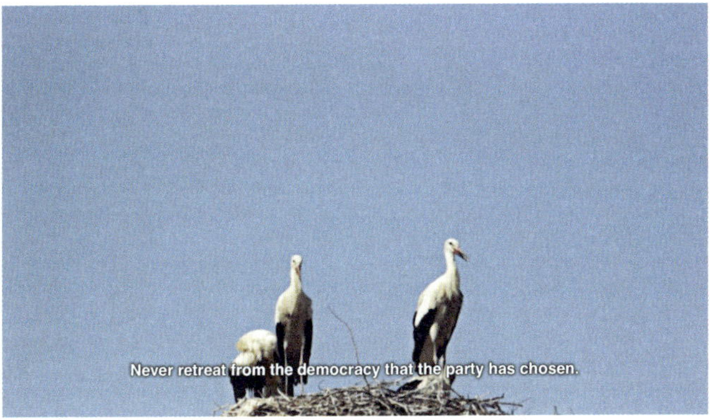
Never retreat from the democracy that the party has chosen.

Image Credits

Cover, pp. 122–23 Lord Allenby with his pet Marabou stork in Cairo, date unknown. Courtesy of King's College Archive, Allenby family, and Liddell Hart Centre for Military Archives.

p. 4 Lieutenant General Sir E. H. H. Allenby, K. C. B., promoted for distinguished service in the field. Photo: Adolphus Tear.

p. 5 Photograph of a white stork in profile. Manipulated by Heba Y. Amin. Photo: Andreas Trepte.

pp. 32–39 Courtesy of Matson (G. Eric and Edith) Photograph Collection.

p. 40 A tweet about the capture of Menes on the *Time* Twitter news feed, and a statement from National Conservation Egypt about its response to the capture of the stork.

p. 41 Newspaper headlines in response to the capture of Menes the stork in 2013.

pp. 42–43 Collage courtesy of the artist.

p. 44 Lithograph of a *Pfeilstorch* ("arrow stork") by Friedrich Lenthe, 1822.

p. 45 Taxidermied *Pfeilstorch* (1822), Zoological Collection of the University of Rostock, Germany. Courtesy of Markus Rack.

pp. 52–57 Courtesy of Haitham Mossad.

pp. 72–73 *Background*, Google map showing the location of Dendera, Egypt. Map data © 2020 Google; *top right*, detail of the painted relief ceiling in the Dandarah Temple complex, which is located 2.5 kilometers southeast of Dandarah. Photo: Olaf Tausch; *bottom left*, Wadi Qena, the forward operating base used during Operation Eagle Claw.

p. 75 Photographs of protests during the Iranian Hostage Crisis in 1979. Photo (*bottom*): Marion S. Trikosko.

pp. 76–77 © picture alliance/AP Photo.

pp. 78–79 Courtesy of the National Archives Catalog.

p. 80 *Above*, Julius Neubronner holding a homing pigeon and one of his cameras, 1914; *below*, a homing pigeon wearing Neubronner's camera. Courtesy of Kronberg Archive.

p. 81 Aerial images taken with Julius Neubronner's camera, 1908.

p. 82 Mohamed Abdel Ghani el-Gamasy, Egyptian Field Marshal and Commander in Chief of the Egyptian Armed Forces, during the 1973 Arab–Israeli War.

p. 83 Last preparation before first tactical mission across Suez Canal in 1969. Standing: Major Shabtai Brill from the Israeli intelligence corps, innovator of the tactical UAV.

p. 84 Gunsight footage of the July 12, 2007, Baghdad Airstrike, leaked to the public in 2010 as *Collateral Murder* by the online whistleblower site WikiLeaks.

p. 85 The "SmartBird" developed by the German industrial control and automation company Festo.

pp. 86–87 © picture alliance/AP Photo/Shah Khalid.

pp. 88–89 Screengrab from the computer game *Syrian Warfare* (2017). © Valve Corporation.

pp. 106–9 Pages from *The War Illustrated*, 1918. Collection of the artist.

p. 110 Copy of letter of surrender of Jerusalem, signed by the mayor Hussein Salim al-Husseini, December 9, 1918.

p. 111 Proclamation of Martial Law in Jerusalem in English, French, and Italian, signed by Allenby, General, December 11, 1917.

p. 112 The surrender of Jerusalem by the mayor, Hussein Salim al-Husseini (holding the white flag), to the British on December 9, 1917. Courtesy of the Library of Congress.

pp. 114–15 Spread from Vivian Gilbert, *The Romance of the Last Crusade: With Allenby to Jerusalem* (New York: D. Appleton, 1923).

p. 116 Entry of Field Marshal Allenby, Jerusalem, December 11, 1917, with Governor Borton Pasha reading the proclamation in English.

p. 117 *Above*, Field Marshal Allenby accepts surrender of Jerusalem officials, January 1, 1917; *below*, illustration of Allenby entering Jerusalem. Magic-lantern glass slide, 1940. Collection of the artist.

p. 118 Page from *The War Illustrated*, date unknown. Collection of the artist.

p. 119 Page from *Illustrated London News*, January 19, 1918. Collection of the artist.

p. 120 Page from *The War Illustrated*, January 4, 1919. Collection of the artist.

p. 121 Page from *The Sphere*, January 19, 1918. Collection of the artist.

p. 124 Courtesy of British Pathé.

p. 125 Clipping from an unknown newspaper sent to the artist in 2016. Collection of the artist.

pp. 126–27 Courtesy of King's College Archive, Allenby family, and Liddell Hart Centre for Military Archives.

pp. 128–29 Photo: Bettmann Archive/Getty Images.

pp. 140–51 Stills from Heba Y. Amin, *As Birds Flying*, 2016. Video, 7:11 min. Courtesy of the artist.

pp. 158–59 Photographs of Allenby, cropped and manipulated by Heba Y. Amin.

Acknowledgments

We would like to thank the following people for their valued support and input into the research and production of this volume:

Allenby Family
Mohamed Abdel Raouf
Samiha Allouba
Andreas Bick
Wayne Daly
Goethe-Institut, Ankara
Gergő Halmos
Adam Harvey
Adel Iskandar
King's College Archive
Liddell Hart Centre for Military Archives
Haitham Mossad
Moviemento, Berlin
Nature Conservation Egypt
Noor A. Noor
Markus Rack
Laura Poitras
Livia Tarsia in Curia
Puruli Kültür Sanat, Ankara
Raphael Wolf
Moiz Zilberman

Contributors

Heba Y. Amin is a Berlin-based visual artist, researcher, and lecturer who looks at the convergence of politics, technology, and architecture. Her works and interventions have been covered by the *New York Times*, *Guardian*, *Intercept*, and CNN. She has had recent exhibitions at the 10th Berlin Biennale, MAXXI Museum, Rome, 15th Istanbul Biennale, 12th Dak'Art Biennale, Dakar, and the Museum of Modern Art, Warsaw. Amin is the cofounder of the Black Athena Collective and a current Field of Vision fellow (NYC). She also has an extensive repertoire in public speaking. Furthermore, Amin is one of the artists behind the subversive graffiti action on the set of the television series *Homeland*, which received worldwide media attention.

Anthony Downey is Professor of Visual Culture in the Middle East and North Africa (Birmingham City University). He is Cultural Lead on a four-year AHRC-funded research project (2020–24) focusing on cultural practices, education, and digital methodologies in the Middle East. He sits on the editorial boards of *Third Text* (thirdtext.org) and *Digital War* (digital-war.org), and is the series editor of Research/Practice (Sternberg Press, 2019–ongoing). Recent and upcoming publications include *Unbearable States: Digital Media, Cultural Activism and Human Rights* (forthcoming, 2021); *Displacement Activities: Contemporary Art and the Refugee Condition* (Sternberg Press, 2021); and *Critique in Practice: Renzo Martens' "Episode III: Enjoy Poverty"* (Sternberg Press, 2019).

Adam Harvey is a Berlin-based researcher and artist focused on computer vision, privacy, and surveillance. His previous projects on surveillance, including "CV

Dazzle" (camouflage from face recognition), "Anti-drone Burqa" (camouflage from thermal cameras), and "MegaPixels" (interrogating face-recognition information supply chains), have been covered widely in publications including the *BBC*, *Der Spiegel*, *Washington Post*, *New York Times*, *Wired*, and *Financial Times*.

Adel Iskandar is a Middle East media scholar, postcolonial theorist, and Assistant Professor of Global Communication at Simon Fraser University in Vancouver, Canada. He has authored several works, including *Egypt in Flux: Essays on an Unfinished Revolution* (AUC Press/Oxford University Press, 2013) and *Media Evolution on the Eve of the Arab Spring* (Palgrave Macmillan, 2014). Iskandar's engaged participatory research includes supporting knowledge production through scholarly digital publishing such as *Jadaliyya*, of which he is coeditor, and academic podcasting such as *Status*.

Haitham Mossad is an ornithologist and member of Nature Conservation Egypt, and has worked for the Aswan Protectorate Office, Ministry of Environment. He graduated from the Environmental Science Department, Aswan University, and studied geography at University of Glasgow, Scotland. Mossad is currently a PhD student at Wageningen University & Research, the Netherlands.

Laura Poitras is an American filmmaker and journalist. She has received numerous awards for her work, including the 2015 Academy Award for Best Documentary Feature for *Citizenfour*, about Edward Snowden; her first film, *My Country, My Country*, was nominated in the same category in 2007. Her reporting on NSA surveillance received the George Polk Award for National Security journalism and shared the 2014

Pulitzer Prize for public service. She is a MacDowell Colony Fellow, a 2012 MacArthur Fellow, the creator of Field of Vision, and one of the initial supporters of the Freedom of the Press Foundation. Her most recent film, *Risk*, premiered at the Cannes Film Festival in May 2016. Her first solo museum show, “Astro Noise,” took place in 2016 at the Whitney Museum of American Art.

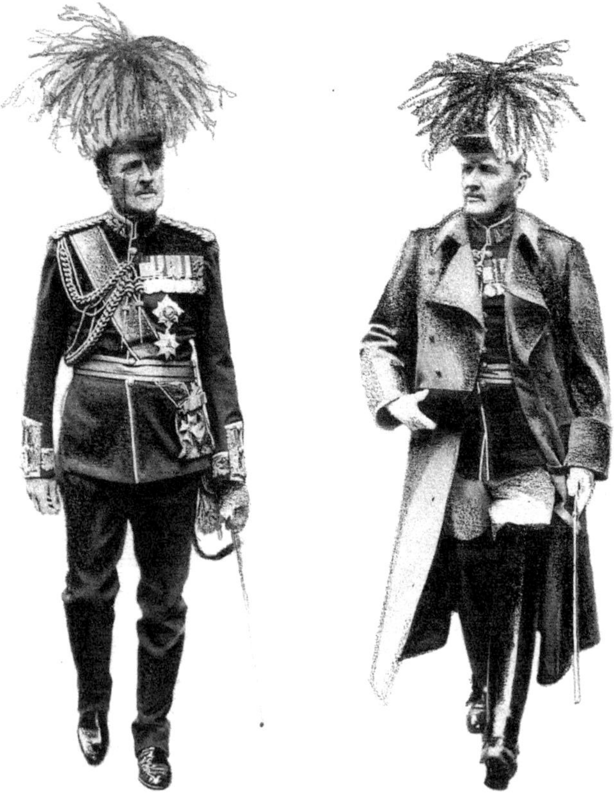

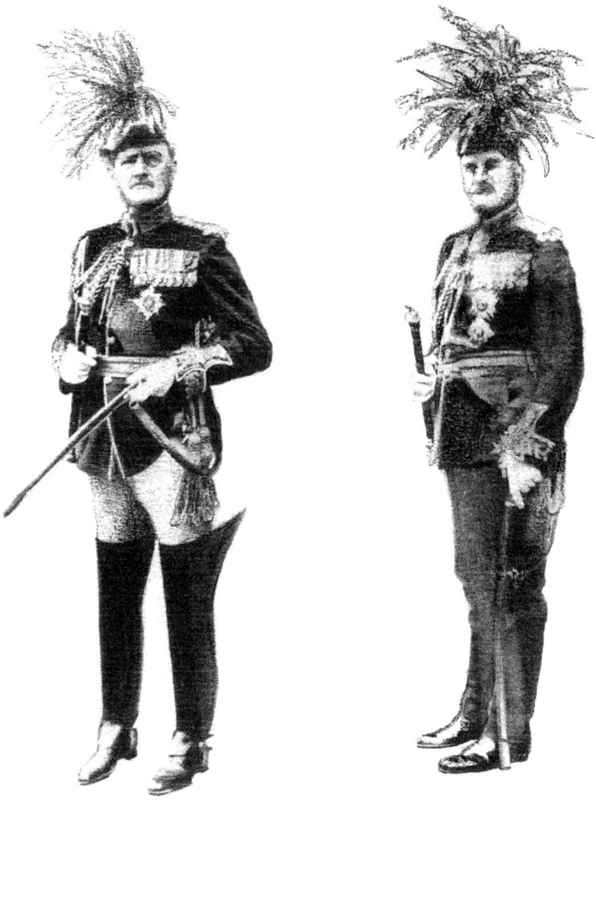

Research/Practice 02

Heba Y. Amin
The General's Stork

Published by Sternberg Press

Editor: Anthony Downey
Managing Editor: Niamh Dunphy
Proofreading: Siobhán Dunphy
Image Research: Raphael Wolf
Design: Daly & Lyon
Printing: Kösel GmbH & Co. KG

ISBN 978-3-95679-478-0

Distributed by The MIT Press, Art Data, and Les presses du réel

Sternberg Press
Caroline Schneider
Karl-Marx-Allee 78
D-10243 Berlin
www.sternberg-press.com